Words of Life

THE BIBLE DAY BY DAY WITH THE SALVATION ARMY

EASTER EDITION JANUARY-APRIL 2002

Hodder & Stoughton
LONDON SYDNEY AUCKLAND
AND THE SALVATION ARMY

British Library Cataloguing in Publication Data
A record for this book is available from the British Library

ISBN 0 340 75702 7

Printed and bound in Great Britain by
Omnia

Hodder & Stoughton
A Division of Hodder Headline Ltd
338 Euston Road
London NW1 3BH

EASTER CALL

I'm glad I didn't hear
that chilling God-forsaken scream
that split the rocks and tore the hearts
of those who loved him best.

I wish I'd heard his call of triumph
that signalled the death of death
and gave me freedom
to walk hand-in-hand with God again.

This is the call I hear –
along no Galilean waterfront
but in the crowded cities of men's lostness
to live out his life, write his hope
and make his love touchable.
This call I hear and in responding
find my own death and resurrection.

Barbara Sampson

CONTENTS

MAJOR BARBARA SAMPSON WRITES...

I have been writing this Easter edition in the months leading up to Christmas. It is a strange feeling to be out of step with the rest of the world. My heart has been full of Easter while all around me is Advent. Just a few months ago, I was full of Advent while all around me was August!

A focus on Easter through the Advent lens has been a rich experience. The two events, Jesus' birth and death, are celebrated only a few months apart, but there's a huge leap from the softly sleeping baby in the manger to the bloodied man nailed to the cross. My grandson asks, 'How did Jesus grow up so quickly?'

As we walk this Easter journey with our hearts so recently filled with Christmas, let us remember that Easter is the reason for his coming. What the cradle began, the cross completed. In a word, he was born to die. At Christmas we recall how God handed over his son in human form to the waiting arms of Mary and Joseph. At Easter Jesus was handed over to betrayal, denial, trial and crucifixion. But this is not defeat, nor reason to despair. This is the story of our redemption. This is why he came!

As Jesus stood before Pilate, just before his sentencing to death, he said, 'For this ... I was born, and for this I came into the world' (*John 18:37*).

May there be blessing for you in this Easter edition as we journey with Jesus towards Jerusalem and all that awaited him there.

ABBREVIATIONS USED

AV   Authorised (King James) Version
GNB   Good News Bible
NIV   New International Version
NRSV   New Revised Standard Version
RSV   Revised Standard Version

SASB   *The Song Book of The Salvation Army*, 1986

RUTH

Introduction

The book of Ruth is a story of God's steadfast love and redemption. The book is only eighty-five verses long, but some form of the word 'redeem' is used twenty-three times. Naomi is the main recipient of redemption in the story; her daughter-in-law, Ruth, the instrument of that redemption.

The story is like an extended parable, beautifully crafted and shaped, with a purposeful repetition of words and phrases to highlight themes and underline ambiguities. It could be simply told this way:

Bethlehem   Naomi   Husband   Two sons   Fullness
Famine   Moab   Death and loss
Foreign wives   Ruth   Orpah
Grief upon grief
Bitter loss
Poverty
Empty
Faithful love
Return to Bethlehem
Ruth gleans   Boaz notices
Uncover   Cover   Proposal   Grain poured out
Kinsman-redeemer   Responsibility   Negotiate   Recover
Blessing   Marriage   Baby   Fruitful   Fullness   Jesus Redeemer

Although set in ancient Israel, the story has a thread that runs right to our day, for it contains the news of God's steadfast love (*hesed*), the faithful, patient, persistent, never-giving-up-no-matter-what love of God that will not let us go.

TUESDAY 1 JANUARY

The Emptying

Ruth 1:1–5

'In the days when the judges ruled, there was a famine
in the land . . .' (v. 1, NIV).

An artist would paint the beginning of the story of Ruth with a series of bold, dark brush strokes. The story is set 'in the days when the judges ruled', a time of religious apostasy and moral depravity in the history of Israel when there was no ruler in the land, not even God, and 'everyone did as he saw fit' (Judg 17:6). Famine grips the land. Bethlehem, the 'House of Bread', has no bread. A man named Elimelech, his wife Naomi and two sons, who are Ephrathites ('fruitful') from Bethlehem, move to live in the land of Moab, east of the Dead Sea, where there is food.

The very mention of the name of Moab would have a negative sound. When the Israelites were travelling in the wilderness after their escape from bondage in Egypt, their encounters with the Moabites were either hostile (Num 22) or shameful (Num 25). Moab was one of the nations that had oppressed Israel during the period of the judges (see Judg 3:12). While intermarriage between Israelites and Moabites was not forbidden, no Moabite – or his sons to the tenth generation – was allowed to 'enter the assembly of the LORD' (Deut 23:3).

Fleeing famine, the family runs into death. First Elimelech dies, leaving Naomi a single parent of two sons in a foreign land. The two sons, Mahlon and Kilion, whose names in Hebrew are suggestive of their short lifespan, eventually take Moabite wives, Orpah and Ruth, but within ten years both sons die. For Naomi, the land of Moab, which promised sustenance and escape, has become a place of death and loss. She is left (v. 5) with neither husband nor sons. She has only two young daughters–in–law, both of whom are foreigners and childless.

This introduction to her story, not unlike the beginning of the story of Job, paints a bleak picture of Naomi facing loss upon loss. But this picture of emptiness will not be the end of the story.

Pray today for someone you know who begins this new year in sadness, loss or emptiness.

WEDNESDAY 2 JANUARY

The Turning

Ruth 1:6–14

'Then Naomi said to her two daughters-in-law, "Go back, each of you . . . It is more bitter for me than for you" ' (vv. 8,13, NIV).

Upon hearing that 'the LORD has come to the aid of his people' and that bread has returned to the 'House of Bread', Naomi decides to go home. Her daughters-in-law set out with her, but along the way Naomi stops and tries to persuade them to go back to Moab. A widowed woman would normally return to her father's house (*Gen 38:11*), but Naomi's urging to each of them to go back to her mother's house is her way of encouraging them to look for new husbands and thus find 'rest' (*v. 9*).

She blesses them, saying, 'May the LORD show kindness to you.' The word 'kindness' is a translation of the word *hesed*, which is one of the most important attributes given to God in the Hebrew Scriptures. It means 'steadfast love' and describes the patient, persistent love of God that will not let us go. It is the Old Testament equivalent of the New Testament word 'grace' and is a word that will appear and reappear in this story. Naomi implies that both her sons' brides have been kind and loyal to their husbands and to her, and she now trusts that God's *hesed* towards them will be shown in the provision of new husbands.

The young women both protest, insisting that they would rather continue with Naomi than return to their own homes. She counters their protest by referring to the customary practice of levirate marriage. If an Israelite man died before producing any offspring, his brother was expected to marry the widow and to allow the first-born son of that marriage to carry on the name of her first husband. Naomi knows that she cannot provide new husbands for these young women. Unlike the land around Bethlehem, she has no expectation of ever being fruitful again.

Orpah obeys her mother-in-law's instruction and turns back to her mother's house, weeping as she goes. But Ruth clings to Naomi. This young Moabite woman will herself become the embodiment of *hesed*, God's steadfast love.

'Give thanks to the LORD, for he is good; his love (hesed) endures forever' (Psalm 118:1).

3

THURSDAY 3 JANUARY
'Your God, My God'

Ruth 1:15–22

'But Ruth replied, "Don't urge me to leave you or to turn back from you. Where you go I will go, and where you stay I will stay. Your people will be my people and your God my God"' (v. 16, NIV).

As Orpah leaves to return to her own people, Naomi once again urges Ruth to do likewise. Naomi, sensible and practical, can see no personal benefit for Ruth in staying with her mother–in–law, nor is she legally required to do so. But Ruth's response is prompted by love and loyalty, not by logic. In words that can only be described as 'full of grace', she speaks her intention to Naomi. 'I will go ... I will stay... I will die ... I will be buried ... Your people, my people ... Your God, my God.'

It seems that Ruth has already committed herself to the Lord by whom she swears (v. 17). She has already committed herself to the family into which she married. These non–negotiable loyalties explain her determination to 'cling' to Naomi (the old word 'cleave' of Genesis 2:24, as in a marriage relationship), and her indignation at being asked to return to her family of origin.

Her speech is an act of *hesed*, showing love and loyalty over and beyond what would be expected. It is also an act of courage, for she is moving to an unknown people who despised her people, while knowing that there will be little hope of marriage among them. Naomi is silenced by Ruth's expression of determination and the women travel on together.

At their arrival in Bethlehem, the 'whole town' is stirred. 'Naomi!' the women gasp. 'Is it really you, Naomi?' Their reaction may be in surprise at her unexpected appearance after more than ten years, or it may suggest that the weight of grief and loss has changed her almost beyond recognition (cf. *Job 2:12*). 'Don't call me Naomi ("pleasant"),' she replies. 'Call me Mara ("bitter").' She complains that she went away full, with a husband, two sons and a promising future, but she has come back empty. Both her former fullness and her present emptiness have been caused by the Almighty. In her bitterness, Naomi neither introduces nor acknowledges her daughter–in–law. But the mention of the beginning of the barley harvest hints that something fruitful may be about to happen!

4

FRIDAY 4 JANUARY
The Contagion of Kindness

Ruth 2:1–16

'Now Naomi had a relative on her husband's side from the clan of Elimelech, a man of standing, whose name was Boaz' (v. 1, NIV).

Back home in Bethlehem, Naomi slumps into depression and passivity, but Ruth leaps into action. She asks permission to go to the fields to find enough grain to keep them alive. The law of Moses instructed landowners to leave what the harvesters missed so that the poor, the alien, the widow and the fatherless could gather the gleanings (see *Lev 19:9–10; 23:22*). Ruth fits all these categories so has every right to glean.

'As it turned out', she began to glean in a field belonging to Boaz who was from the clan of Elimelech, Naomi's husband. This 'happening' is not attributed to God, but it is not hard to see that it is more than a coincidence. The exact relationship between Boaz and Elimelech is unclear, but Boaz is described as a 'relative' in the sense of a distant acquaintance and not, at this stage, as someone with any family obligations to the women. He is 'a man of standing', obviously a wealthy landowner. His name means 'in him is strength', and the way he greets his workers suggests that he is a godly man.

Noticing Ruth, Boaz asks his foreman to tell him who she is. She is identified as being 'the Moabitess who came back from Moab with Naomi'. Boaz approaches Ruth and welcomes her to his field, telling her to 'stay' with the other servant girls. He uses the same word that was used to describe the way Ruth 'clung' to Naomi (*1:14*). He has already told his men not to bother her and he tells her where to get water when she is thirsty.

'Why take notice of me, a foreigner?' she asks. His reply indicates that he has been told the whole story of her *hesed*, loving loyalty and kindness to her mother-in-law. This is the contagion of kindness. The *hesed* of Ruth draws out the very same quality from Boaz. Love gives birth to love. Kindness creates kindness. Ruth bows before Boaz and says, 'May I continue to find favour in your eyes' (*v. 13*). Indeed she will!

SATURDAY 5 JANUARY
The Kinsman-Redeemer

Ruth 2:17–23

' "The LORD bless him!" Naomi said to her daughter-in-law. "He has not stopped showing his kindness to the living and the dead" '
(v. 20, NIV).

As Ruth heads home from the fields, she carries with her the grain she has gathered and the leftovers from her lunch (v. 14). Her gleaning for the day has resulted in an unusually large amount of barley – an ephah, which is about half a bushel. When Naomi hears the news that it is Boaz who has taken such notice of Ruth (cf. v. 10), the grief-stricken places of her heart begin to thaw. Her speech moves from cursing to blessing. She had seen God as her harsh Judge, the one who took her to Moab full and brought her home empty. Now she pictures him as a Giver of Life. She blesses Boaz for his kindness (hesed). This outburst of blessing and gratitude indicates a moment of awakening hope for Naomi. It is a crucial turning point in the story.

Naomi then explains to Ruth that Boaz is a close relation to the family, one of their kinsman-redeemers. The word 'redeemer' is 'one who takes responsibility for' another, keeping life and love alive, the family together and the community intact. Members of the extended family were called to be redeemers for those whom life had left helpless. So a kinsman-redeemer would provide for an heir for a brother who had died (Deut 25:5–10), redeem land that a poor relative had sold outside the family (Lev 25:25–28), redeem a relative who had been sold into slavery (Lev 25:47–49) and avenge the killing of a relative (Num 35:19–21).

Naomi encourages Ruth to 'go with' (the word 'cling' again, as in 1:14) his women workers, so that she will not be bothered by anyone. This sounds like simple motherly advice but Naomi's concern may well contain a tinge of self-interest. Now that Boaz has 'taken notice' of Ruth, Naomi may be beginning to see that a marriage between her kinsman-redeemer and her daughter-in-law could result in a solution to her own problems.

To reflect on
Ruth had shown kindness beyond the call of duty to her mother-in-law.
Boaz has shown kindness to Ruth.
The power of hesed is in full swing!

SUNDAY 6 JANUARY
In the Arms of the Shepherd

Psalm 28

'Save your people and bless your inheritance; be their shepherd
and carry them for ever' (v. 9, NIV).

Psalm 28 begins with the psalmist making his individual prayer to the Lord 'my Rock'. It ends with his prayer on behalf of his people, praying that God will be 'their shepherd'. The movement from 'my' to 'their' is significant. Prayer that is only between 'me-and-God' but neglects others is out of balance, like a three-legged stool with one leg missing.

The psalmist is praying in a desperate situation, although it is unclear just what his circumstances are. With urgency in his tone, he begs God to hear him and not be silent. He lifts his hands in prayer, perhaps toward the holy of holies, the place of God's presence, or in a gesture of receiving an answer to his prayer.

He paints a graphic picture of the wicked – evildoers who speak sweetness with their words but slander in their hearts. His prayer that they get what they deserve is not a matter of personal revenge but rather divine justice (see Ps 94:2). Completely self-absorbed, the wicked show by their deeds that they want no part in the goodness and order of God, and so they leave God no choice but to 'tear them down and never build them up again' (v. 5).

Between verses 5 and 6 something changes for the psalmist. Perhaps a word has been spoken by the priest. The worshipper lifts his heart in joyful praise to God for his answer. He thanks God for his strength, his help, his salvation (vv. 7–8), benefits of God's reign that his people already experience. But he prays that even yet God will 'save' and 'bless' his people (v. 9). This prayer reminds us of Jesus' words when he taught his disciples about the kingdom that is both already here and still coming (see Luke 17:21; 22:18). Saving and blessing – two of the things God does best!

To reflect on
As we begin this new year with all its unknowns, one thing we can be sure of is that we are carried in the arms of the Great Shepherd.

MONDAY 7 JANUARY

The Uncovering

Ruth 3:1–5

'When he lies down, note the place where he is lying.
Then go and uncover his feet and lie down. He will tell you
what to do' (v. 4, NIV).

Ruth continues to live with her mother-in-law while going each day to glean in the fields of Boaz. The fruits of her gleaning would provide little more than subsistence for the two. Widows in Israel were the poorest of the poor. They were customarily taken advantage of or ignored. Being both a widow and a foreigner, Ruth would have no right to property or a home of her own.

As the harvest season comes to a close, Naomi moves into action. Her hopes may have been raised by the attention that Boaz paid to Ruth when they first met, but there seems to have been no further action from him. She speaks to Ruth about her need for security and, in the next breath, mentions the name of Boaz. She obviously has marriage in mind. She tells Ruth to wash and perfume herself and to put on her best clothes. This would be the normal pattern for the end of a period of mourning (see *2 Sam 12:20*) or for the preparation of a bride for her wedding (see *Ezek 16:10*). Ruth is to go down to the threshing-floor where Boaz will

be spending the night, both for the protection of his grain, and to await his turn at threshing. When he lies down to sleep, she is to go and uncover his feet and lie there.

To modern ears, this sounds a rather seductive thing to do. In the Hebrew text the words 'to know', 'to lie down', 'to sleep' and 'uncover' all have sexual overtones. Even the word translated 'feet' here is more accurately translated 'lower body'. Is Naomi deliberately putting Ruth into a situation where she may be taken advantage of? Worse, are they both schemers, out to trap a wealthy relative into doing something against his will?

The text does not explain. We know only the hopeless situation that Ruth faces if something is not arranged for her, and Naomi's confident faith in the power of the kinsman-redeemer to help a destitute relative. Obediently, Ruth does as she is told.

TUESDAY 8 JANUARY
The Covering

Ruth 3:6–13

' "I am your servant Ruth," she said. "Spread the corner of your garment over me, since you are a kinsman-redeemer" ' (v. 9, NIV).

At the threshing–floor everyone is asleep. Everyone, that is, except Ruth who lies in stillness at the feet of Boaz. In the middle of the night he suddenly wakens, startled to find a woman lying there. When he asks who she is, Ruth identifies herself as his servant, then asks Boaz to spread his cover over her.

At his first encounter with Ruth, Boaz blessed her by the God of Israel, 'under whose wings you have come to take refuge' (2:12). Ruth now uses that same expression to Boaz. In asking him to cover her 'under his wing' she is in fact proposing marriage (see *Ezek 16:8*). By adding 'since you are a kinsman-redeemer', she is also reminding him of his responsibilities.

Boaz responds to Ruth's request for marriage, saying that he will do all that she asks (v. 11). He then responds to her request for redemption, saying that it depends on one factor outside his control. He tells her of an even closer relative who will have a prior responsibility as kinsman-redeemer, and who therefore must be consulted first. He commends her in that this current act of loyalty or kindness (*hesed*) to him is even greater than her former expression of loyalty to Naomi.

Boaz's words in verse 10 indicate that Ruth could have remedied her own situation by getting any one of the young men to marry her. But only marriage to one of Elimelech's closest relatives could address the needs of Ruth's family. He swears that, one way or another, he will see to the recovery of what was lost after the deaths of Elimelech, Mahlon and Kilion.

He agrees to marry Ruth, assuring her that the people in the community know that she is a woman 'of noble character'. This is the feminine equivalent of how Boaz himself was described, 'a man of standing' (2:1). So there is an equal regard for them both, even though he is a wealthy landowner, and she a destitute foreign widow.

This is surely the outworking of the hesed love of God!

WEDNESDAY 9 JANUARY
An End to the Emptiness

Ruth 3:14–18

'He gave me these six measures of barley, saying, "Don't go back to your mother-in-law empty-handed" ' (v. 17, NIV).

In the dim morning light Boaz urges Ruth to go before she is recognised. This may be to protect her reputation as 'a woman of noble character' (v. 11), or to protect his own. He pours six measures of barley into her shawl. His reasons for doing this are unclear. The significant amount of grain might be a bride price or a marriage settlement. It might be the price for the option to buy the parcel of land that belonged to Elimelech (4:3). It could be an expression of blessing and reassurance to Naomi. Certainly that is how the older woman receives it.

When Ruth arrives home, she tells Naomi all that Boaz has done for her. She shows the generous gift of grain and reports Boaz's words about not going back empty-handed. Naomi must indeed have felt that her days of emptiness are coming to an end. Her earlier lament that the Lord had taken her away full but brought her back empty (1:21) is at last put to rest. Just as the land around Bethlehem has become fruitful again after the famine, so too Naomi's barren life is now suddenly gaining a new and unexpected fruitfulness. She receives the grain as a sign from Boaz that the matter of the more immediate kinsman–redeemer is about to be settled.

Yet there is more than a tinge of suspense in the air. How can Boaz possibly resolve the matter in a way that caters for both women? The levirate marriage laws stated that if a man dies, his brother should marry the widow and continue the family line. If Boaz had been one of Elimelech's brothers, a marriage to Naomi would not have solved Ruth's problems. Nor would it continue the family line, since Naomi is past the age of child–bearing (1:11). The levirate custom would put no expectation on him to marry Ruth. So just how is the matter to be resolved?

To reflect on
Ruth is told simply to 'wait', which is often the hardest thing of all to do. What do you need to wait for today?

THURSDAY 10 JANUARY
Uncover, Cover, Recover

Ruth 4:1–4

'I thought I should bring the matter to your attention and suggest
that you buy it in the presence of these seated here and in the
presence of the elders of my people. If you will redeem it, do so.
But if you will not, tell me, so that I will know' (v. 4, NIV).

While Ruth is told to sit tight and wait (3:18), Boaz goes out to sit at the town gate. This was the court-house of ancient Israel, the place where many business transactions were conducted and disputes set-tled. Boaz calls the next of kin 'my friend' but uses a Hebrew idiom that suggests the man's name is not important, presumably because he was not willing to redeem. Some-one has called him 'So-and-So'.

Boaz tells So-and-So about the parcel of land that Naomi is selling, the first time that such a piece of land is mentioned. It could be that Naomi owns the land but is having to sell it because of her destitute state. A kinsman-redeemer would be duty-bound to buy any land that was in danger of being sold outside the family. Alternatively, it could be that Elimelech sold the land before the family moved to Moab. By law Naomi holds the right to redeem or buy it back, but because of her poverty she is dep-endent on a kinsman-redeemer to do it for her. In this case, it would be the right of redemption that she is selling. Or it could be that So-

and-So, as Elimelech's closest rela-tive, had claimed the land when the family moved to Moab and has been cultivating it during the years of their absence.

Whichever explanation is correct, Boaz reminds So-and-So that it is his duty to buy (or pay for) the field that legally belongs to Elimelech's heirs. He says, 'I thought I should bring this matter to your attention.' Literally the Hebrew says, 'I thought I would uncover your ear.' On the threshing-floor, Ruth had 'uncov-ered' Boaz and asked him to 're-cover' (redeem) that which was lost. Boaz now 'uncovers' the ear of this kinsman-redeemer and challenges him to recover (redeem) the land that belonged to Elimelech. In re-sponse to this open challenge in the presence of ten elders and, no doubt, a crowd of interested spec-tators, So-and-So states his will-ingness to do what duty demands.

To reflect on
'Cover, uncover, recover' – these words
are a picture of redemption.

FRIDAY 11 JANUARY
The Blessing

Ruth 4:5–12

'Then Boaz said, "On the day you buy the land from Naomi and from Ruth the Moabitess, you acquire the dead man's widow, in order to maintain the name of the dead with his property" '
(v. 5, NIV).

'Oh, by the way,' says Boaz, hearing So-and-So's declaration that he will redeem Naomi's land. 'There's one more thing you need to know. We're not just talking about land in this deal. If you buy the land, you also need to take responsibility for Ruth the Moabitess and produce a son to keep Elimelech's line alive. And if you don't, I will!'

The laws concerning redemption of land stated that land sold to a redeemer 'will remain in the possession of the buyer until the Year of Jubilee' (*Lev 25:28*). It would then be returned to whoever had a legitimate claim to its title. Assuming that Elimelech's line would die out, with there being no more sons in the family, So-and-So was willing to redeem the land. But if Boaz provided Elimelech and Mahlon with an heir, then So-and-So and his heirs would eventually lose both the land and the price they had paid to purchase it. He had not considered this possibility and so withdraws his right to redeem. 'Buy it yourself,' he says.

He removes his sandal and passes it to Boaz. This was the symbolic way of renouncing one's property rights and passing them to another (see *Deut 25:7–10*). Holding the sandal aloft, Boaz turns to the ten elders and the watching crowd. He declares publicly that he has made both the land and Ruth his own. He begins and ends his speech with 'Today you are witnesses!' The people respond, 'We are witnesses', and the legal transaction is completed.

With one voice the witnesses pronounce a threefold blessing on Boaz and Ruth. 'May Ruth produce as many offspring as did Rachel and Leah. May you produce children in Ephrathah and be famous in Bethlehem. May your descendants be as many as Judah and Tamar.' It is a blessing of fruitfulness, and while it is addressed to Boaz, it recalls the women who have played an essential part in maintaining the continuity of the family line in the past.

To reflect on
Consider how Ruth's story has moved from emptiness to fullness.

SATURDAY 12 JANUARY

The Completion

Ruth 4:13–22

'Then Naomi took the child, laid him in her lap and cared for him. The women living there said, "Naomi has a son" ' (vv. 16,17, NIV).

The beginning of Naomi's story was painted in bleak colours of loss and emptiness. The conclusion is splashed with bright colours of joy and fullness. Ruth and Boaz are married and, by the grace of God, she conceives and gives birth to a son. The women of the town welcome this child as Naomi's redeemer, but they see his significance as far more than merely retaining the family property. His birth represents the redemption of Naomi from the emptiness that had engulfed her with the loss of her husband and sons. Just as they had received her back from Moab in an empty, bitter state (1:20,21), now they rejoice at the reversal that this child represents. Naomi's life has gone from fullness to emptiness and back to fullness again.

They declare that Ruth is of greater value than seven sons. Seven was considered a number of completeness (cf. Job 1:2), and to have seven sons was considered the greatest blessing that any family could have. Although she was herself bereft, widowed and foreign, Ruth's selfless devotion, her steadfast love (hesed), has moved Naomi from bitterness to blessing, from emptiness to fullness, from barrenness to fruitfulness. The child, Obed, is Naomi's redemption in person, for 'he will renew your life and sustain you in your old age' (v. 15). So Naomi takes the child and cares for him. She is aged, well past child-bearing herself, but through Ruth she has obtained an heir in place of Mahlon. Her heart joins in the song of praise and thanksgiving, 'Naomi has a son!'

The chapter concludes with a genealogy, which begins with Perez, whose birth was similarly from a union based on the levirate practice (see Gen 38:27–30). Matthew's genealogy names Rahab as the mother of Boaz. Like Ruth, Rahab was a non-Israelite woman who chose to align herself with Israel and Israel's God. Thus Obed, the 'root' of David's family tree and ancestor of Jesus, had both a Moabite mother and a Canaanite grandmother. It is not ethnic or racial purity that guarantees our salvation. This is the story of God's redemption!

SUNDAY 13 JANUARY
In His Temple All Cry 'Glory!'

Psalm 29

'The voice of the LORD is over the waters; the God of glory thunders, the LORD thunders over the mighty waters' (v. 3, NIV).

Psalm 29 is considered to be the oldest of the psalms. It is a hymn in praise of the King of creation whose majesty and power are both seen and heard in nature. Following the opening invitation to praise the Lord, there is a poetic description of a thunderstorm. The Canaanite people considered that their god Baal was responsible for weather and fertility. Thunder was thought to be Baal's voice.

But this psalm affirms that it is God who is the Lord of nature. He is the one who is in control of the storms and rain that are so vital for harvest and survival. His is the voice that sounds out across the waters. His is the voice that causes the thunderstorm. His is the voice that uproots trees and shakes the earth. His name 'the LORD' is sounded four times; in the body of the psalm it is heard ten times. 'The voice of the LORD' is repeated seven times. These are the numbers of fullness or completion. God's strength is all-powerful, God's sovereignty – not Baal's – is absolute.

Someone commenting on Psalm 29 makes a link between the composer of this psalm and General William Booth. Just as Booth determined that the devil should not have all the best tunes, and so adapted the popular music of his day for the expression of worship, so too the psalmist has adapted the popular understandings of his world and used them to express the worship of his God.

God is the Lord of nature, sovereign over the human environment, providing life-giving rain for his world. But he is also Lord of history, sovereign in human affairs, daily giving strength and protection to his people and blessing them with his peace. He alone is to be acknowledged as the divine King. Let all in his temple – his world – cry 'Glory!' on this day of worship.

All good gifts around us
Are sent from Heaven above;
Then thank the Lord, O thank the Lord
For all his love!
Matthias Claudius SASB 935

MARK 7–10

Introduction

The portion of Mark's Gospel from 7:24 to 10:52 records a significant new stage of Jesus' ministry. Up to this point, the calling and sending out of the first disciples, his teaching and healing ministry and early controversy with the religious leaders have all taken place around Galilee. The encounter with a Syro–Phoenician woman (7:24) marks a new beginning – his ministry to the Gentiles.

These chapters are filled with cameos of Jesus healing, feeding, warning, rebuking, embracing, predicting. He is still a man on the move, but the word 'immediately' does not appear so often. There is now a steadier, more resolute and purposeful sound in his tread. He is 'on the way' to Jerusalem and to his death. But as he goes he is, as always, attentive to the cries of distress of those who need his healing touch, such as a deaf and mute man, a plucky Gentile woman who will not take 'no' for an answer, a couple of blind men.

Woven through his healing activity are three predictions of his coming suffering and death. But the disciples, those who travelled most closely with him 'on the way', seem more deaf and more blind than the people who are brought to him for physical healing. While Jesus speaks of suffering, his disciples squabble over status. While he describes his death, they dispute about their positions in his coming kingdom. At the very centre of this section, his question, 'Who do you say I am?' meets with a response from Peter that shows he knows the name 'Christ', but still has little idea of what that name, 'Anointed One', really means.

Over the next four weeks, I invite you to come with me into Mark's world. Let us join Jesus and his straggling disciples 'on the way' to Jerusalem.

MONDAY 14 JANUARY
A Reluctant Healing?

Mark 7:24–30

'As soon as she heard about him, a woman whose little daughter was possessed by an evil spirit came and fell at his feet' (v. 25, NIV).

Jesus travels to the region of Tyre and finds a place to stay, away from the demands of the crowd and his ever-watchful opponents. But his presence cannot remain secret for long. When word gets out that he is in the area, a woman whose daughter is a victim of an unclean spirit seeks him out. Mark describes the woman as a Greek, born in Syrian Phoenicia; in other words, a Gentile pagan. The Jews considered Gentiles to be impure simply because they were Gentiles.

Jesus dismisses her appeal for help with what seems like an insult: 'First let the children eat all they want . . . for it is not right to take the children's bread and toss it to their dogs.' His word 'first' suggests that her time will come but, for the moment, she has no right as a Gentile to jump the queue to receive anything from him.

But she will not be put off. She understands his riddle, that 'the children' represent Israel and 'the dogs' represent the Gentiles. She knows that she has no claim on grace, that she is last in line, unclean and excluded. But her desperation for her child will not

let her take 'no' for an answer. She asserts that even the 'little dogs' under the table get to eat the 'little crumbs' that the children drop. She is not asking for a banquet, just a little crumb of Jesus' power for a little girl. Jesus faces her challenge and says, 'You're right, of course. Go on your way – your daughter is healed.' She goes in faith just as she came, and finds the child lying in bed, the demon gone.

This is the scandal of grace. This woman was outside the community of faith but her desperation gave her faith, and what she asked for. She speaks today for all those whom human prejudice would hold at arm's length, but whom God longs to embrace with his love.

To reflect on
'It is the possession of a joyful and genuine humility that alone enables us to receive grace.'

Bernard of Clairvaux

TUESDAY 15 JANUARY
Healing the Deaf Mute

Mark 7:31–37

'The man's ears were opened, his tongue was loosened and he began to speak plainly' (v. 35, NIV).

Jesus travels through Sidon and then back through the district of the Decapolis to the Sea of Galilee. The long detour may have been to maintain secrecy but even in Gentile territory the news of his presence spreads quickly. A crowd brings him a deaf and speechless man, begging Jesus to heal him. Jesus has no desire to make his healing work a spectator event so he takes the man away from the crowd. He cannot speak to the man because he is deaf, so he acts out what he intends to do. He begins by putting his fingers in the man's ears, symbolic of opening them. Next, he spits and touches his tongue, symbolic of loosening it. Then he looks up to heaven, the source of his power, and sighs deeply, a gesture of prayer. He speaks a simple healing word, 'Ephphatha', which Mark translates 'Be opened!'

Immediately the man's ears are opened and his tongue loosened, his speech now normal. Jesus orders 'them' not to say anything, a strange command to someone who has just been given his voice! Jesus can command storms, spirits and sicknesses, but his orders for people to keep silent fall on deaf ears. What Jesus does is so sensational that it is hopeless to try to hush it up. But while they chatter in excitement about what Jesus has done, its deep significance escapes them. Even the disciples are still a long way from hearing and understanding what Jesus is doing. They need a miracle similar to the one the deaf man has received.

The crowd's amazed reaction, 'He even makes the deaf hear and the mute speak' (v. 37), echoes Isaiah's promises that God will open the eyes of the blind and the ears of the deaf and loosen the mute tongue (Isa 35:5–6). God's promises to restore all creation are beginning with Jesus. The surprise is that this restoration occurs in Gentile territory.

To reflect on
Beethoven died with the words, 'I shall hear in heaven.' Unless we hear God's words on earth, we will never hear them in heaven.

WEDNESDAY 16 JANUARY
Yet Another Miraculous Feeding

Mark 8:1–10

'His disciples answered, "But where in this remote place can anyone get enough bread to feed them?"' (v. 4, NIV).

Jesus is still in the region of the Decapolis when another miraculous feeding takes place. A Gentile crowd this time, they are a long way from home and have listened to his teaching for three days without food or complaint. Jesus has compassion on them and is fearful that, if he sends them home without food, they will faint on the way. As with the first miraculous feeding (6:34–44), he instructs the disciples to give them something to eat. In the first incident, the disciples had worried over the great expense of buying bread for such a huge crowd. This time, their anxiety is because there is no place nearby for the crowd to buy bread for themselves.

They have come so recently from the first miracle, but they have clearly forgotten it. Looking at their own meagre supplies, they are convinced that the task is impossible. 'But where . . . ?' they ask. The answer to their question is obvious: from Jesus. How could they forget so quickly? Why was the memory of that first blessing and breaking and feeding not etched forever on their minds?

Could it be that in that first incident, the crowd was Jewish and so the miracle was acceptable? But this time, as if with spiritual blinkers on, they wondered how a Gentile crowd could be fed. One gets the impression of a group of disciples, those who presumably knew him best, struggling to keep up with him. It's as if everything is happening too quickly, and their question, 'Who is this man?' (4:41), becomes ever harder to answer. They could accept him as a redeemer for the Jews, in the style of Moses or David. But this kind of feeding miracle, one that encompasses Gentiles in the blessing of God, can be seen only as a sign of the end-time reign of God. If this is so, they must have wondered, could Jesus be the redeemer of more than just the people of Israel? Could he in fact be the Redeemer of the whole world?

To reflect on
What do you think?

THURSDAY 17 JANUARY
Signs and Sighs

Mark 8:11–21

'Aware of their discussion, Jesus asked them: "Why are you talking about having no bread? Do you still not see or understand? Are your hearts hardened?" ' (v. 17, NIV).

After the feeding of the crowd, Jesus sets sail with his disciples to the region of Dalmanutha. Out of nowhere, it seems, a group of Pharisees appears, challenging him to give them a sign from heaven. He sighs deeply in dismay at their challenge and retorts that no sign will be given. He himself, of course, is God's sign from heaven, standing in flesh before them, but they are spiritually blind and cannot recognise him.

The disciples are just as blind. In yet another boat incident they make it obvious that they have completely failed to understand. In the first incident (4:35–41), Jesus calmed the storm and rebuked them for their lack of faith. At that time they whispered, wide-eyed, to each other, 'Who is this?' In the second boat scene (6:45–52) they were terrified when Jesus came walking over the water towards them. Mark says they were amazed, for their hearts were hardened. Now in this third boat incident Jesus rebukes them for quarrelling over their lack of bread and accuses them of having hardened hearts, blind eyes and dull hearing. He warns them about the yeast of the Pharisees and Herod.

In the Old Testament, yeast or 'leaven' symbolised corruption and the infectious power of evil. Leaven was produced by holding back a piece of the previous week's dough and then adding juices to it to cause fermentation. But the leaven could easily become tainted and infect the rest of the dough and then the next batch. The Pharisees, steeped in religiosity, and Herod in his wickedness, held one thing in common – their obstinate refusal to believe in spite of the evidence. Jesus warns his disciples not to fall into the same trap of unbelief.

Their anxiety over where their next meal will come from holds them back from looking up and seeing what Jesus has already done in their midst. They have distributed bread to thousands, but they fail to recognise that they have the bread of life (*John 6:35*) sitting with them in the boat.

To reflect on
What does your unbelief prevent you from seeing?

FRIDAY 18 JANUARY
Healing a Blind Man

Mark 8:22–26

'They came to Bethsaida, and some people brought a blind man and begged Jesus to touch him' (v. 22, NIV).

As Jesus and his disciples arrive in Bethsaida, people bring a blind man to him, asking for his healing touch. Once more Jesus avoids making the healing a spectacle by leading the man away from the village. Jesus puts saliva on the man's eyes and then asks if he can see anything. The man looks up and says he can see people, but they look like walking trees. This blindness is obviously stubborn and hard to cure.

Jesus then repeats the procedure, placing his hands on the man's eyes. No word of healing is spoken, just a touch. The man opens his eyes wide, his sight is restored, and he can see all things clearly. The miracle shows Jesus' power to heal even the most difficult cases. Jesus tells him to go home but orders him not to go into the village.

This blind man's healing occurs between two examples of the disciples' blindness (8:14–21, 31–33). Just as the healing of this man seemed difficult and took two attempts, so the healing of the disciples' spiritual blindness will come only gradually and with difficulty.

In spite of their close company with Jesus and all they have observed – his healing of physical ailments, the casting out of evil spirits, feeding the thousands, walking on water – yet they have failed to recognise him as the Messiah, sent and empowered by God. In spite of all they have heard by way of his teaching and his colourful parables of the kingdom, they have failed really to understand. Like students in school, they need to go over it all again, to see and see clearly. They need to listen again, so that they hear and hear clearly.

The next major section of Mark's Gospel (8:27–10:52) shows Jesus avoiding the villages and crowds as he heads steadily towards Jerusalem. His concentration now is on healing the disciples' deafness and blindness, for which more than one course of treatment is required.

To reflect on
The disciples seem so slow to understand, but are we – are you – so different?

SATURDAY 19 JANUARY
Who do You Say I Am?

Mark 8:27–30

' "But what about you?" he asked. "Who do you say I am?" '
(v. 29, NIV).

The breathless pace of Mark's account from town to town, miracle to miracle, slows down now to a steady walk. The word 'immediately', used thirty-two times to this point, is scarcely used from now on. Jesus now leads his disciples 'on the way'. Their classroom is no longer the boat or the hillside, but the journey itself. This incident takes place at the centre of Mark's Gospel, and acts like a hinge between the first half, where Jesus' power is so prominent, and the second half, where his vulnerability becomes predominant.

In this scene, Jesus is 'on the way' to Caesarea Philippi. This city lay on the border between Israel and Gentile territory and was well known for its worship of Greek gods. Against this pagan backdrop, Jesus asks his disciples two probing questions. In response to the first, 'Who do people say I am?', they report his favourable ratings. His opponents think he is possessed by Beelzebub (3:22); his family think he is out of his mind (3:21); his fellow citizens from Nazareth dismiss him as just one of them (6:3), but Joe Bloggs, the man in the street, holds a good opinion of him. Most people in fact think he is a prophet sent by God, in the style of John the Baptist or Elijah.

Jesus hears their answer and then asks the real question, 'But what about you? Who do you say I am?' Until this point they have only called him 'Teacher' (4:38), but Peter now gives an answer that makes sense of all they have witnessed, 'You are the Christ.'

Well done, Peter! The scales have fallen! All has been revealed! But no, Jesus neither confirms Peter's confession nor praises him for his insight. Instead, he orders him to tell no one, just as he had commanded the demon to be silent (1:25). Knowing the name 'Christ' does not mean that Peter understands what the Christ will do. For all of them, there is still much to learn.

To reflect on
If Jesus were to ask you that same question today, how would you answer?

SUNDAY 20 JANUARY

Praying to Live – Living to Praise

Psalm 30

'O LORD my God, I will give you thanks for ever' (v. 12, NIV).

Psalm 30 is clearly a song of thanksgiving, but what is not so clear is whether it is the celebratory prayer of an individual who has just recovered from serious illness, or a communal song of celebration at a feast of dedication. The psalm in fact may have featured in a variety of settings. Of significance for worshippers in this day is that while the psalm is a prayer, the substance of the prayer is praise.

The psalm opens with a picture of God in action. The psalmist uses the word 'extol' (meaning 'to lift up') to praise God, for God has lifted him (as in drawing water from a well) out of the depths. He has brought him up from the grave and spared him from going down into the pit. Whether the deliverance has been from an illness or from enemies who threatened him, it is certain that God has heard the psalmist's desperate cry for help.

In response to this deliverance, the psalmist invites the congregation to join him in praise and thanksgiving. He has learned something deeply significant through his experience – that the reason for his existence is to praise God. God's commitment to life and blessing means that the ultimate end of human suffering is not 'weeping' but 'rejoicing'.

As he looks back over his former distress and at how God has delivered him, he realises that prosperity had made him feel invincible. He was as strong as a mountain, vigorous and victorious, but sickness had shattered his self-confidence and brought him to the edge of his mortality. In a new awareness of God as the source of his health, and praise the purpose for his existence, he determines that from now on – for ever in fact – he will be thankful. Praise will be his way of life. For the psalmist, wailing has indeed been turned into dancing, the drab garb of mourning exchanged for the multicoloured garments of joy.

To reflect on

The psalmist prays to live and lives to praise. Could the same be said of you?

22

MONDAY 21 JANUARY
The First Prediction

Mark 8:31–33

'He then began to teach them that the Son of Man must suffer many things and be rejected by the elders, chief priests and teachers of the law, and that he must be killed and after three days rise again' (v. 31, NIV).

I recall as a youngster the excitement that my friends and I felt when we found out the first name of one of our teachers. In those days, a teacher was addressed as 'Mr . . .' or 'Miss . . .' and a respectful distance was maintained. But finding out their first name was like discovering an intimate secret, and the cause of much whispering and giggling. Suddenly they were human after all!

Peter may have felt that addressing Jesus as 'the Christ' (v. 29) gave him an intimate insight into this companion whom they hardly knew at all. His glorious moment of faith, however, is short-lived. Jesus rebukes him, telling him not to speak about the matter and then explaining that it is necessary for the Son of Man to suffer, be rejected and then killed. This prediction is spoken 'plainly' (v. 32), not in parables (4:33).

Peter is stunned (the word 'gobsmacked' comes to mind!) and plunged into an uncomprehending daze. Jesus explains that this is all part of God's plan of salvation. Only after these things have happened at the hands of the elders, chief priests and teachers of the law, will vindication come about. Peter takes Jesus aside and rebukes him for even suggesting that the Messiah will have to suffer. Peter and the others have seen his amazing powers to still the sea and unclean spirits, heal the sick with a touch or just a word, feed thousands from a meagre lunch, and forgive sins. How could such an obvious Messiah with such obvious powers be rejected and killed? It is quite unthinkable.

Once again Jesus turns and rebukes Peter, calling him 'Satan'. Peter may think the Messiah will be immune from suffering, but Jesus knows he will be Messiah by way of suffering. Mark's point is clear. A disciple must do more than know Jesus' title. That is only the first step in following Jesus on the way.

To reflect on
Satan uses one disciple, Peter, to try to turn Jesus away from death. He uses another disciple, Judas, to lead him into death.

TUESDAY 22 JANUARY
Saving and Losing

Mark 8:34–9:1

'For whoever wants to save his life will lose it, but whoever loses his life for me and for the gospel will save it' (v. 35, NIV).

Jesus now turns to the crowd, drawing them into his teaching. The demands and expectations of discipleship are open to anyone willing to accept his conditions. He offers three demands (v. 34), an explanation (vv. 35–37), a warning (v. 38) and a promise (9:1).

Jesus insists that the first requirement of following is to deny oneself and one's own plans and ambitions. Second, a follower must take up a cross. A cross was a familiar image. The Romans made the condemned carry their own cross to the place of execution. The historian Cicero described death on the cross as a slave's punishment, a cruel, disgusting penalty, the worst of extreme tortures. In calling disciples to carry their cross, Jesus is not thinking of a gold-plated cross worn around one's neck, but is calling them to be willing to follow and obey even to the point of giving their lives, just as he himself will do.

His third demand is for them to follow the way he has chosen, not the way they would choose for themselves. Jesus does not call people to armchair Christianity,

with a remote control at hand ready to switch off anything unpleasant. He calls disciples to follow his way, his example, his cross-bearing. His explanation for such radical following sounds paradoxical. To save one's soul, one has to lose it. If we give up our lives for his sake and the gospel, we will be given the only life that counts – life from God.

He warns the crowd that everyone will have to give an account of their life when the Son of Man comes as Judge. Confessing him will not make life easy, but it will save us from God's judgment. He then concludes this first lesson on the requirements of discipleship with a promise. The suffering will not go on for ever. The resurrection of the Son of Man (v. 31) and his coming in glory (v. 38) will take the horror out of the cross.

To reflect on
'When Christ calls a man he bids him come and die.'

Dietrich Bonhoeffer

WEDNESDAY 23 JANUARY
A Glimpse of Glory

Mark 9:2–8

'After six days Jesus took Peter, James and John with him and led them up a high mountain, where they were all alone. There he was transfigured before them' (v. 2, NIV).

On the seventh day after Peter's confession and Jesus' warning of his coming suffering, Jesus takes Peter, James and John up a high mountain. These three were an inner circle for Jesus, the first to be called (1:16–20), the first in the list of disciples' names (3:16–17), the ones who watched the raising of Jairus' daughter (5:37–43). It will be these three whom Jesus takes aside with him in Gethsemane (14:33), where they will witness his agony and distress. For now they witness his glory.

This incident, called the transfiguration, has a number of parallels with Moses' meeting with God on Mount Sinai (Exod 24; 34:29–35). Jewish traditions understood Moses' ascent of Sinai as an enthronement. In similar style, Jesus' transfiguration reveals that he is a king. While the disciples are still trying to make sense of his predictions about suffering, here they see a glimpse of the glory that will follow his resurrection. The unearthly white glow of his clothing is but one of the signs of resurrection (see 16:5; Matt 13:43). Jesus speaks of the resurrection of the Son of Man as they come down the mountain.

In the midst of this visual spectacle, Elijah and Moses appear conversing with Jesus. These two great Old Testament leaders – Moses who was Israel's greatest deliverer, and Elijah who was the greatest of the prophets – are 'endtime' figures. Their presence with Jesus suggests that the coming of the kingdom of God is near (1:15).

Peter longs to hold on to the moment. Enough talk of suffering, he thinks, let's make this glorious experience last for ever! He suggests putting up three shelters, tents of hospitality, which will act as a kind of messianic headquarters on the mountain. Mark comments that Peter does not know what to say, because he is afraid (v. 6). Peter continues to see things from a human perspective, rather than from God's. Moses and Elijah disappear and Jesus stands alone before the disciples. He says nothing, but the voice of God speaks clearly, telling the fearful three to listen.

Let that be your focus today – 'Listen!'

25

THURSDAY 24 JANUARY
Another Day, Another Hilltop

Mark 9:9–13

'As they were coming down the mountain, Jesus gave them orders not to tell anyone what they had seen until the Son of Man had risen from the dead' (v. 9, NIV).

As the disciples come down the mountain with Jesus, he commands them to keep quiet about what they have seen and heard. For once, the command for silence is obeyed, even though they are still puzzled about the reference to the Son of Man's resurrection from the dead. How can the Messiah be rejected and suffer? Jesus offers no explanation, except that it is written and it is necessary. The disciples have already witnessed that the Son of Man has authority to forgive sins, to raise the dead, to heal the afflicted. They have heard him declare that the Son of Man is Lord of the Sabbath, that he will be enthroned at the right hand of power and will come in clouds with great glory. But they cannot yet comprehend that the same Son of Man will suffer betrayal, humiliation and death. For Jesus, the glory and the suffering go hand in hand. In fact, his suffering will be far greater than imagined, but so will his glory.

For those with eyes to see, this experience on the mountain of transfiguration has parallels with another day on another hilltop:

The glory of the mountain of trans-figuration has been for private viewing.

The suffering of the cross will be a public spectacle.

On this mountain Jesus has the company of two prophets, Moses and Elijah.

On Golgotha, it will be two thieves.

On the mountain of transfiguration, his garments have shone.

On Golgotha, his clothing will be stripped off him.

On the mountain of transfiguration, three male disciples see his glory.

At the cross, three female disciples will watch his suffering.

On the mountain of transfiguration, Elijah appears.

As he hangs on the cross, one of the bystanders will taunt, 'Let's see if Elijah comes to take him down.'

On this mountain a voice from the cloud declares that Jesus is the Son of God.

After his death, a Roman centurion, one of his executioners, will announce the same thing.

To reflect on
'He was crucified in weakness, yet he lives by God's power' (2 Cor 13:4).

26

FRIDAY 25 JANUARY
A Fragment of Faith

Mark 9:14–27

'Immediately the boy's father exclaimed, "I do believe;
help me overcome my unbelief!" ' (v. 24, NIV).

As Jesus heads down the mountain he finds the everyday world of discord and demons waiting for him. The other disciples are arguing with the teachers of the law. When Jesus asks what the argument is about, a man in the crowd steps forward and explains that he had brought his demon–afflicted son to Jesus for healing. The boy is mute and tormented by seizures that throw him to the ground, cause him to foam at the mouth and grind his teeth, and make him rigid. 'I asked your disciples to drive out the spirit,' he says, 'but they could not.'

The disciples' failure and the noise of their dispute make Jesus cry, 'O unbelieving generation . . . how long shall I put up with you?' He knows that his time is short. Will they ever learn? Immediately he takes action, calling for the boy to be brought. As he comes, the boy is thrown into a convulsion. Jesus does not address the spirit that possesses the boy but speaks directly to the father, asking if he has faith. The boy's torment and the disciples' failure could have robbed the father of all faith, but

there is a fragment left. 'If you can do anything,' he says. But Jesus' ability to act is not in question. This is a struggle of the father's ability to believe. He pleads for help just as he is, a doubter.

In response, Jesus does battle with the spirit as it lashes the boy in one last frenzy. The convulsion leaves the boy looking as if he is dead, but Jesus seizes his hand and raises him up. He drives out the evil spirit and gives the boy new life. The father's fragile faith in the strong power of Jesus is answered.

Dwight L. Moody said there are three kinds of faith:

- *Struggling faith, like someone in deep water, desperately swimming.*
- *Clinging faith, like someone hanging to the side of a boat.*
- *Resting faith, like someone safely in the boat and able to reach out and help others get in.*

27

SATURDAY 26 JANUARY
The Reason for the Power Failure

Mark 9:28–29

'After Jesus had gone indoors, his disciples asked him privately,
"Why couldn't we drive it out?" ' (v. 28, NIV).

The exorcism scene at the foot of the mountain is followed by a debriefing session indoors. The disciples know they failed the father and his tormented son, but they are puzzled as to why. Jesus responds simply, 'This kind can come out only by prayer' (v. 29).

'Prayer? Did you say "prayer", Jesus? We didn't hear you pray as you watched that boy in his convulsion.' Once again the disciples are slow to understand. The prayer Jesus is talking about is not a matter of words, nor a formula, but prayer as relationship, the close and enduring relationship with God that he knows, and longs for his disciples to know. To add to their puzzlement is the memory of their recent success at driving out spirits (6:13). Why could they do it then but not now? Was it their technique that failed, or did they forget an essential ingredient in the exorcism formula?

Jesus' answer makes it quite clear that the driving out of evil spirits has nothing to do with formulas or techniques. The power to cast out evil does not belong to them, but to God. That power must be received each time from him through the living relationship of prayer. The cause of their power failure was simply that they had inadequate faith and insufficient prayer. Their prayers were as mute as the tongue of the afflicted boy. Now they must learn from their failure that all healing comes from God.

Henri Nouwen says that prayer is 'a way of being empty and useless in the presence of God and so of proclaiming our basic belief that all is grace and nothing is simply the result of hard work' (*The Living Reminder*). As modern-day followers of Jesus, our diaries tell us that we are too busy to pray. Prayer becomes a luxury, something to do on an unexpected day off work or on a retreat. But Jesus calls us to prayer, not as a thing to do, but as a way of life.

To reflect on
How will you respond to that call to prayer today?

SUNDAY 27 JANUARY
In Your Hand is My Future

Psalm 31

'In you, O LORD, I have taken refuge' (v. 1, NIV).

The first line of Psalm 31 sum-marises the message of the whole psalm and of many of the psalms in this great songbook. In trusting his life to God, the psalmist has found a place of refuge, an un-shakable rock, a strong fortress. His whole life depends on God who delivers, turns, comes, saves, leads, guides, frees and redeems.

The psalmist speaks his trusting words, however, against a back-ground that is painted with dark splashes of fear and foreboding. He speaks of the trap that has been set for him, his affliction, the an-guish of his soul, the enemies who conspire against him, and the neighbours who hold him in con-tempt. Throughout this psalm words of trust alternate back and forth with words of petition or complaint. 'I turn my life over to you,' he says, using words that Jesus spoke from the cross at the moment of his death (*Luke 23:46*). The apostle Stephen, martyred for his faith, spoke similar words as he died (*Acts 7:59*). It is said that several great saints of the church – Jerome, Martin Luther, John Knox – also died with the words of Psalm 31:5

on their lips. Psalm 31 can teach us how to die.

Just as importantly, Psalm 31 can teach us how to live. Jesus trusted his spirit to God, not only as he died, but every day of his earthly life. He was the supreme example of a servant living in the light of God's face (presence) and unfail-ing love (*v. 16*). Like the prophet Jeremiah, the psalmist discovered that living in God's presence also meant living in the world where enemies and terror pressed in on every side. Yet in that 'besieged city', that tight place, God's wonderful love had been shown to him (*v. 21*), leading him out (as in the Exodus) to a spacious place (*v. 8*). This psalm then is a call to belong to God in both living and dying.

To reflect on
Because of God's faithfulness and un-failing love, we who hope in the Lord have every reason to be strong and take heart (v. 24).

MONDAY 28 JANUARY
The Second Prediction

Mark 9:30–32

'He said to them, "The Son of Man is going to be betrayed into the hands of men. They will kill him, and after three days he will rise" '
(v. 31, NIV).

Leaving Caesarea Philippi, Jesus begins his last tour through the region of Galilee. He wants to keep his movements quiet now for his public ministry is coming to an end. The insatiable crowds have had their day. They have seen enough of his healing and deliverance ministry and heard enough of his teaching to know that a new day of God has dawned. And his future does not rest in the hands of the admiring crowds. The success of his ministry belongs to this fragile group of disciples, with all their inadequacies, who will carry his gospel to the world. He needs privacy to continue teaching them about the death that God requires of him, and about what he requires of them.

For the second time, he speaks of his coming suffering and resurrection (see 8:31). Once again the significance of his announcement passes them by. They are silent, uncomprehending and afraid to ask him what it all means. They may be afraid of being rebuked if they say anything, as Peter was (8:33), or they may prefer to deny the whole matter in the hope that it will simply prove untrue. Denial is, after all, one of the early responses to grief, and at this stage it is an understandable way for them to deal with the fearful things that Jesus is saying.

As they get closer to Jerusalem, however, fear will increasingly control their reactions to the events he predicts (14:50–52, 66–72; 16:8). Having told them earlier that he will suffer and be rejected and killed (8:31), he now adds that he will be betrayed into the hands of men. They might well worry over who it is that will betray him, but instead they argue about which one of them ranks the highest (vv. 33–34). Resolute and lonely, Jesus presses on. All he has to rest his saving task upon is this group. There is no 'Plan B', no alternative scheme to swing into action, should these followers fail.

To reflect on
Even now, 'Christ has no hands but our hands, to do his work today.'

TUESDAY 29 JANUARY
Who is the Greatest?

Mark 9:33–37

'Sitting down, Jesus called the Twelve and said, "If anyone wants to be first, he must be the very last, and the servant of all" '
(v. 35, NIV).

When they reach Capernaum, Jesus asks the disciples what they had been arguing about on the way. They respond with an embarrassed silence. Once again, he has caught them in a dispute. As Jesus walks resolutely towards his humiliating death, his ragtag followers have been pushing and shoving behind him, their hearts set on glory and greatness.

Jesus shows how serious this matter is by sitting down to teach them. He had recently spoken a paradox to them – that saving meant losing and losing meant saving (8:35). Now he speaks another: 'If anyone wants to be first, he must be the very last, and the servant of all.' This paradox is an even greater puzzle to the disciples. They have visions of grandeur, not of being servants.

To reinforce his words, Jesus, the ever-creative visual artist, places a little child in their midst and says, 'Whoever welcomes one of these little children in my name welcomes me.' Jesus was not commending the obedience, trust or innocence of a child, but rather emphasising the child's insignifi-

cance. In Jewish society a child had no power, no status and few rights. A child was dependent, vulnerable, completely under the authority of its father. So Jesus chooses such a one to represent those who are needy and lowly. If you want to be great, he tells them, then you should offer humble, loving service to those who are insignificant, with no ability to pay back what they are given. Jesus then adds to the mystery by saying that when his followers serve those who are without power or status, they are in fact receiving Jesus himself, and the one who sent him.

His words reach from that house in Capernaum right into our homes today. Do you know someone who is forgotten, overlooked, insignificant? Someone who has no influence, no title, no priority? Believe it or not, that person is important to God, as precious as a dearly loved child.

To reflect on
Look for an opportunity today to reach out to such a person with the love of Jesus.

WEDNESDAY 30 JANUARY
Not Against Means For

Mark 9:38–40

'Whoever is not against us is for us' (v. 40, NIV).

Jesus has just rebuked the disciples for their self-seeking. Now he rebukes them for their exclusive attitude. John proudly announces that they saw someone casting out demons in his name and told him to stop. The reason? 'Because he was not one of us.' He was not on our team, Jesus, not wearing our logo, not doing things the way we do them! Their reaction to this unnamed exorcist is ironical. The disciples have recently failed to cast out a demon, and here they are obstructing someone who is successful, but not one of them. Jesus surprises them by rebuking them rather than commending them for their careful screening process.

In the ancient world, exorcists used the names of whatever deities they thought would work. Jesus' explanation for encouraging the exorcist's success in this account is practical rather than theological. He argues that no one can use his name to do a miracle and then speak evil of him. Anyone who recognises the power of Jesus' name will not accuse him of working by Beelzebub, as the teachers of the law from Jerusalem have done (3:22).

Jesus opens the door wide to include on his team any and all who are not against him. His disciples have not caught on yet, but Jesus knows they are engaged in a life-and-death struggle against evil, and he is prepared to accept anyone who is willing to join the fight. Such open-ended tolerance will trouble anyone who is more intent on keeping the lines clear as to who is in and who is out than on winning the war against the enemy. The enemy then becomes anyone who is 'not one of us'. The disciples want to sing:

If you're in (with us), then you're in
But if you're out, you're out!

God's mission in the world is far bigger than we are. Other believers may worship differently, use different language, emphasise different non-negotiables of the faith but the call for all Christians is to have the same attitude that was in Christ Jesus (see *Phil 2:1–5*).

That's a call to cooperation, not competition!

THURSDAY 31 JANUARY
Stumblings and Saltiness

Mark 9:41–50

'I tell you the truth, anyone who gives you a cup of water in my name because you belong to Christ will certainly not lose his reward' (v. 41, NIV).

While John worries about the exorcist who is not on their team, Jesus shifts attention to an act of compassion. He promises that anyone who gives a cup of cold water to his followers will be rewarded. This most basic expression of hospitality sounds insignificant, a little like the child (v. 37) or the sparrow (Matt 10:29–31) that are easily overlooked by others but noticed and loved by God. For the disciples there will be days of hardship and persecution ahead (see 13:13) when a cup of cold water given in kindness will do far more than quench their thirst.

In contrast to this promise of reward is the threat of severe judgment if they cause a little one – a child or a person with a fragile faith – to fall into sin. Jesus uses the language of exaggeration to make his point. They would be better off to drown at the bottom of the sea with a millstone around their necks.

He then speaks a list of warnings concerning their need to be watchful for the potential evil that lies within them. If your hand or eye or foot causes you to stumble into sin, then remove it, chop it off, do radical surgery. His words are not to be taken literally but they are to be taken seriously. In a society where it was considered preferable to be deformed or disabled than to be dead, Jesus applies this principle to the spiritual life of his followers. If doing things with the hands or watching things with the eyes or going places with the feet leads you into sin, then they need to be dealt with firmly, decisively. Dealing with them now will avoid judgment later. Jesus at times deliberately used harsh, scandalous imagery to warn his disciples that their lives are in constant danger, from within and without.

'Have salt in yourselves,' he concludes. To a group of men who so recently have argued about who was the greatest, Jesus' words about cleansing salt urge them to be a people whose dealings with others are characterised by purity, peace and fellowship.

FRIDAY 1 FEBRUARY

A Test Question

Mark 10:1–12

'Some Pharisees came and tested him by asking, "Is it lawful for a man to divorce his wife?" ' (v. 2, NIV).

Two recent reports in our local newspaper:

- The young couple stand at the altar and pledge their lives together 'so long as our love shall last'.
- The photographer asks for a 'divorce deposit' because of the increasing number of people separating before the wedding photos are paid for.

The question of divorce is as complex in this age as it was in Jesus' day. As Jesus travels from Capernaum to Judea, into the area governed by Herod Antipas, the crowds flock to hear him and the Pharisees see their opportunity to test him. John the Baptist had been imprisoned and then beheaded for rebuking Herod Antipas for his unlawful divorce and remarriage to Herodias (6:17–18). The Pharisees may have hoped that Jesus' response to their question would result in a similar fate for him. 'Is it lawful for a man to divorce his wife?' they ask. It is a loaded question, motivated by hostility. They have no desire to offer pastoral care to someone who is divorced. Interested in rights, not responsibilities, their whole approach to the law is, 'What can we get away with?'

Jesus' question in response uncovers their hard, sinful hearts: 'What did Moses command you?' With ease they quote the Mosaic regulations concerning the divorce process. Moses permitted divorce, provided the husband gave his wife a certificate of divorce (Deut 24:1–4). But knowing what Moses permitted is not the same as knowing what God intended. God's true intentions for marriage, Jesus explains, as found in Genesis 1–2, are for two people, created male and female, to be joined in a one-flesh relationship. No one has any right to break such a God-joined relationship and discard an unwanted spouse like a piece of used goods.

Jesus proclaimed that all relationships in the kingdom of God, whether with spouses, neighbours, children or servants, should stand out as radically different from those in the world. Self-sacrificing love should be the hallmark of a marriage; mercy and forgiveness the gifts offered to someone who fails (see John 4:4–29; 7:53–8:11).

To reflect on
God abandons no one!

34

SATURDAY 2 FEBRUARY
A Matter of Littleness

Mark 10:13–16

'Let the little children come to me, and do not hinder them,
for the kingdom of God belongs to such as these' (v. 14, NIV).

Jesus' concern for the care and acceptance of children immediately follows his statements about marriage and divorce. Some people were bringing little children to him. These 'Mothers of Salem', as we sing at infant dedications, come asking for Jesus' blessing on their children, but are met with stern rebuke from the disciples. Self-appointed body-guards, they continue to act like gatekeepers, wanting to control not only who can use Jesus' name (9:38), but also who can have access to him.

Jesus is indignant at their response and informs the disciples that the kingdom of heaven belongs to such as these. His answer would have shocked them. The attitude of the day was that children were non-persons, with no prestige, no rights, no voice. They were merely commodities, adding nothing to a family's economy or honour. Unwanted children were regularly abandoned at birth, exposed to the elements and left to die. One historian reports that the unscrupulous would often collect such children and raise them to be gladiators or prostitutes or even disfigure them to enhance their value as beggars. Such horrific facts find a sad parallel in today's world of rampant child abuse and appalling forms of child exploitation.

Once again Jesus turns the values of the world upside down as he welcomes and embraces and blesses these little ones, using the moment to indicate that he expects his followers to do the same. In fact, he says, little children have things to teach us about the kingdom. Their powerlessness contrasts sharply with the overbearing disciples who want to push others around. They need to learn not only to minister to such little ones but also to adopt an attitude of littleness themselves. The children represent yet another paradox of the kingdom of God. Little ones are easily pushed aside because they are weak, but God delights in littleness, he blesses the poor in spirit, he works most powerfully in those who know they are weak.

To reflect on
Open hands will receive the kingdom of God more readily than hands full of their own importance.

SUNDAY 3 FEBRUARY
The Blessings of Forgiveness

Psalm 32

'Then I acknowledged my sin to you and did not cover up my iniquity. I said, "I will confess my transgressions to the LORD" – and you forgave the guilt of my sin' (v. 5, NIV).

Church tradition names Psalm 32 as the second of the penitential psalms, the first one being Psalm 6. This psalm is a testimony to the nature and benefits of confession, and to the gracious and forgiving character of God. The psalm begins with two beatitudes that look back to the beginning of the psalter at Psalm 1 and the blessings of the righteous that are described there. Psalm 32 makes it clear that being righteous is not a matter of being sinless but of being forgiven. To be righteous is to receive God's grace.

The psalmist speaks from his own experience but knows that it is the same for all believers. He uses three basic words to cover the whole range of unrighteousness:

- Transgression, meaning wilful rebellion against God;
- Sins, meaning offences which 'miss the mark' of God's standard;
- Iniquity, meaning the destructive effects of disobedience.

All three are evident in his life and the results are very real, even physical, causing his bones to waste away through his unceasing groaning. God is fully willing to forgive him, but first the psalmist must break his grace-rejecting silence. Holding his iniquity inside him is like letting waters pile up behind a dam, creating immense pressure on the wall, but as soon as he makes his confession, the floodgates are opened, the waters subside and the pressures diminish.

At the centre of the psalm, the psalmist expresses his relief: 'You forgave the guilt of my sin.' After the announcement of forgiveness, none of the 'sin' words is mentioned again. God has indeed forgiven and forgotten (Ps 103:12). The psalmist now focuses his attention on those who are godly (v. 6), and on God. Forgiven and surrounded with songs of deliverance (v. 11), he now invites others to sing the same refrain. An unquenchable song of joy belongs to all those who know they are forgiven.

To reflect on

St Augustine is said to have had the words of Psalm 32 inscribed above his bed. He wrote, 'The beginning of knowledge is to know oneself to be a sinner.'

MONDAY 4 FEBRUARY
Heaven is Where the Heart Is

Mark 10:17–22

'Jesus looked at him and loved him' (v. 21, NIV).

From empty-handed children, the story now turns to a young man who comes to Jesus with his hands full of his own goodness. 'Good Teacher,' he says as he kneels, 'from one good man to another, I have a question for you.' He wants to be sure that his goodness will pay off in eternal life but wonders if there is anything he may have overlooked.

Jesus addresses the man with no title and chides him for thinking that anyone but God is good. He directs his attention to the Ten Commandments, listing the ones that govern one's dealings with others:

'Murder?' asks Jesus.	'No problem,' says the man.
'Adultery?'	'Heavens, no!'
'Stealing?'	'Certainly not.'
'Bearing false witness?'	'Never!'
'Defrauding?'	'Absolutely not.'
'Honoured your parents?'	'Indeed I have.'

'You can ask anyone who has known me since I was a boy,' he says. 'I've got a spotless record in all these requirements.' I imagine that Jesus looked at this young man for a long, long moment before speaking. Mark says that 'he looked at him and loved him'. Jesus does not sneer at his claims of having obeyed the law. He doesn't cut him down – tall poppy syndrome – for what he says. But because Jesus loves him, he challenges him directly. The man regards himself as respectably good, but respectably good is not good enough. He lacks one thing and Jesus tells him what to do about it: 'Go ... sell ... give ... come ... follow.'

His wealth has taken first place in this man's life and, like a hand or eye or foot that can lead a follower into sin (9:43–47), it needs radical surgery. God's demands turn out to be far more costly than he bargained for. He was wealthy, but he could not pay the price of letting it all go in order to follow. The rich young man came to Jesus asking what he could do, but he leaves sad because of what he could not do.

To reflect on
Is there something anchoring your soul to this world that needs to be let go?

TUESDAY 5 FEBRUARY
Humanly Impossible, Divinely Possible!

Mark 10:23–27

'It is easier for a camel to go through the eye of a needle than for a rich man to enter the kingdom of God' (v. 25, NIV).

The disciples must have blinked incredulously at the scene that has just played out before them. They see a young man coming to ask about eternal life. He has perfect credentials and deep pockets. He would certainly be a helpful addition on their team and a boost to their meagre funds. But Jesus lets this good man slip away! Unbelievable! Then he astounds them even further by commenting that the rich will have a hard time entering the kingdom of God.

The disciples have grown up with the understanding that wealth was proof of God's favour. The blessings were all listed as far back as Moses. Obedience to God and adherence to his commands guaranteed fruitfulness, productivity, safety and freedom (*Deut 28:1–14*). It was a divine insurance policy. 'If you pay attention to the commands of the LORD your God that I give you this day and carefully follow them, you will always be at the top, never at the bottom' (v. 13). That was their kind of language speaking of their kind of place.

But Jesus has a very different perspective. He regarded possessions as an almost insurmountable obstacle that prevented a person from following God wholeheartedly. He saw wealth as toxic to the soul. The best thing was to invest it in ministering to the poor, the needy, the destitute – those who had no chance of giving any return.

Seeing their reaction, Jesus addresses them, for the first and only time, as 'children', as if to remind them of what he has so recently demonstrated, that they must become like children if they are going to enter the kingdom of God (*v. 15*). He uses a colourful image to reinforce the point that those who are ruled by money cannot be ruled by God. The rich will find coming under God's rule more difficult than trying to squeeze a camel (the largest animal in Palestine) through the eye of a needle (the smallest opening imaginable).

To reflect on
Entering the kingdom of God means submitting to God's rule and allowing him to reign over every aspect of our lives.

WEDNESDAY 6 FEBRUARY
Leaving and Receiving

Mark 10:28–31

' "I tell you the truth," Jesus replied, "no-one who has left home or brothers or sisters or mother or father or children or fields for me and the gospel will fail to receive a hundred times as much in this present age . . ." ' (vv. 29,30, NIV).

Still stunned that Jesus has allowed the wealthy young man to walk away, Peter reminds Jesus that he and the others have given up everything to follow him. Jesus promises that their sacrifice will not be in vain. As in the parable of the sower and the good soil (4:8), their offering will multiply a hundred times over. This is one of the promises of Jesus that cannot be experienced 'from the outside looking in'. From those first disciples to modern-day followers, countless people have discovered that what they received has been far greater than what they gave up in order to follow Jesus.

Giovanni di Bernardone was born into a wealthy family, his father a rich landowner and fabric merchant. The young man would have inherited the family business but war intervened and when he returned from the war, Giovanni had changed. One day he took some fabric and sold it and his horse at the market, and gave the money away. His father was furious and called in the bishop, who ordered the young man to return what he had taken. Giovanni stripped off his clothing, laid it at his father's feet and said, 'Up until now I have called you father. Now I have no father but God.' And so Giovanni di Bernardone, more commonly known as Francis of Assisi, set out on the narrow path of pilgrimage. He wore a threadbare, patched tunic and called those who followed him to live in radical poverty as joyful peacemakers in the world.

For my husband and myself, serving God meant leaving our immediate family in New Zealand. At Chikankata, Zambia, we found that the people we worked and wept, socialised and struggled with, Zambian and expatriate, became our family. Now, many years later, this family is spread right around the world and is living proof for me that this promise of Jesus still stands true.

To reflect on
A wealthy woman who gave up her fortune to set up houses of refuge for abused women said, 'In the women's tears I saw my diamonds again.'

THURSDAY 7 FEBRUARY
The Third Prediction

Mark 10:32–34

'They were on their way up to Jerusalem, with Jesus leading the way, and the disciples were astonished, while those who followed were afraid. Again he took the Twelve aside and told them what was going to happen to him' (v. 32, NIV).

The way that Jesus and his disciples have been taking is now named as the route to Jerusalem. The prophet Isaiah pictured the ransomed of the Lord entering Zion with singing and everlasting joy (Isa 35:10). This struggling, squabbling little band of disciples looks nothing like a victory procession as they follow Jesus to his death. As Jesus builds the highway of the Lord, the disciples, still worried about the pecking order of the procession, trail behind. Mark says they are amazed and afraid. Is it the fear of persecution and suffering that slows their steps? Is it a sense of wonder and amazement at Jesus who seems to know what lies ahead of him, and yet resolutely moves forward to embrace it?

Jesus does nothing to put their fear to rest, but predicts for the third time his imminent death and then resurrection. The details this time are more specific than they were previously (9:31). He will be betrayed to the chief priests and teachers of the law who will condemn him to death and hand him over to the Gentiles, who in turn will mock him, spit on him, scourge him and kill him. The Messiah will suffer indignity and a shameful death. Then three days later he will be resurrected.

His words are plain and clear. He uses no parable, no hidden meanings, no symbolism. But as Jesus draws nearer to his death, his disciples do not draw any nearer to understanding. Each time he speaks to them about his suffering, his words just go 'in one ear and out the other'. It is not that they are slow-witted but rather that he is using language that does not fit their world-view. They have loved the displays of power, the amazing miracles, the glorious achievements, and they want a Messiah who is beyond suffering and death and who will offer them all their heart's desires.

To reflect on
Jesus marches forward, offering to his disciples – then and now – not a way of success, but a way of life.

FRIDAY 8 FEBRUARY
When Will They Ever Learn?

Mark 10:35–45

'To sit at my right or left is not for me to grant. These places belong to those for whom they have been prepared' (v. 40, NIV).

Jesus speaks for the third time of his coming suffering and death, explaining all that he is about to give (vv. 33,34). Immediately it seems, with no appropriate respectful pause, the disciples come with their list of all they want to get. James and John grab his attention first, much to the annoyance of the others (v. 41). The earlier dispute about status and rank among the disciples (9:34) was silenced but not settled.

'Jesus,' they ask, 'let one of us sit at your right and the other at your left in your glory.' In their still-blinkered view, they see Jesus as the Messiah, the coming King, and they want to be the crown princes sitting alongside him on thrones of their own. The new age they look forward to has special privileges for special friends. Since they were two of the first to be called, they want to be first in glory as well.

'When will they ever learn?' went the folk song. 'When will they ever learn?' Maybe these two will learn only when they stand at the cross and watch him die with two criminals crucified alongside him, 'one on his right and one on his left' (15:27). What will they think then of their pleading for those favoured positions?

Jesus answers graciously, 'You don't know what you are asking.' The cup and the baptism – both metaphors for suffering – that he is about to endure will overwhelm him. His glory will be by way of suffering, with no short cuts. Are they ready for that? 'Yes, of course,' they answer glibly. Self-confident, they believe they can endure a little hardship, just a sip of the cup, if Jesus will grant them positions of power. These two, and the others who are indignant that they got their request in first, are still a long way from understanding that greatness is to be found in humble service.

To reflect on

The place of honour in God's kingdom is not at the head of the line but at the end. Where is that place for you today?

SATURDAY 9 FEBRUARY
The Blind Man Sees

Mark 10:46–52

' "What do you want me to do for you?" Jesus asked him'
(v. 51, NIV).

This incident near Jericho is Jesus' last healing in the Gospel of Mark. The shadow of the cross now looms heavily over him, but he can still hear the cries of others in distress. The crowd tries to make the man stop his noise, but Jesus stops for him. He has already shown that no one – a leper, a woman with a haemorrhage, little children, and now a blind beggar – is beyond his care.

Earlier in this chapter, the Pharisees wanted to trap Jesus (v. 2). The rich man wanted eternal security at minimum cost (v. 17). James and John wanted to be kingpins in the kingdom (v. 37). Bartimaeus asked to see again, recognising Jesus as the Son of David and calling him Rabbi. This blind man showed that of all these people he is perhaps the most perceptive of all.

Jesus asks Bartimaeus the same question that he had addressed to James and John (v. 36). 'What do you want me to do for you?' The disciples want to sit on thrones with Jesus and reign with him in triumph. Bartimaeus sits in the dust, makes no request for glory, but cries out of his wretched poverty. He only wants to see. The disciples see Jesus as a Messiah who will bring them mastery and glory; Bartimaeus sees him as the Son of David who brings healing and sight. Jesus cannot grant the disciples' request for power, but he can grant a blind man's request for vision.

'Call him,' Jesus tells the crowd, as he hears the man's urgent cry. This time there is no healing word or gesture, no spittle rubbed in the eyes (see 8:23), just Jesus' response to the man's faith-filled plea. Bartimaeus leaves his cloak, perhaps his sole worldly possession, his begging cloth by day and his blanket by night. With eyes wide open, he follows Jesus on the way.

To reflect on

It is one of the most important questions that God ever asks us. 'What do you want me to do for you?' How would you answer that question today?

SUNDAY 10 FEBRUARY
The Earth is Full of God's Unfailing Love

Psalm 33

'The LORD loves righteousness and justice; the earth is full of his unfailing love' (v. 5, NIV).

Psalm 33 begins as Psalm 32 concludes, in celebration of God's unfailing love. In language of praise, the psalmist calls for songs of praise to be played on the harp and the ten-stringed lyre, with joyful singing and shouting. The reason for this new song of praise is God himself.

He is to be praised for his word (vv. 4–9). In a declaration that recalls Genesis 1, the psalmist describes how God created the world, the heavens, the stars, the waters of the sea, by his spoken word. 'He spoke, and it came to be; he commanded, and it stood firm' (v. 9).

He is to be praised for his plan (vv. 10–12). Creation rests upon the divine word, but history rests upon the divine plan. Human plans and schemes, for all their strength, are subject to divine restraint. In contrast, the Lord's plans are powerful and permanent and are not subject to human restraint. The nation whose God is the Lord is blessed because it is founded upon God's plan, and not on the fickle foundations of human politics.

He is to be praised for his eye (vv. 13–15). With a vision that sweeps the cosmos, God looks down and sees all humankind. His eye rests in love upon individuals as well, as distressed Hagar found in the wilderness when she had run away from Sarai (Gen 16:13).

He is to be praised for his might (vv. 16–19). It is futile to depend on the humanly recognised sources of strength – the size of one's army, the strength of a warrior or his horse. Strong as these forces may be, they are nothing when compared with God. Pharaoh and his army pursued Israel after the Exodus, but it was the Lord who was recognised as the true warrior (Exod 15).

Having led his congregation in praise, the psalmist now concludes on a note of prayer (v. 22). May God's unfailing love that fills the earth now rest upon his people. Amen!

Choose one of these reasons to praise God today.
Make it personal to your situation.
Then do it!

THE VITAL VERBS OF PRAYER
Introduction

I love grammar. The study of languages at school opened for me a world of ablatives, gerunds and subjunctives such as I never knew existed. But I've discovered that there is good grammar and bad grammar. The latter makes me grind my teeth. I mentally correct any wrong spelling I see. I refuse to go into a shop that has spelling mistakes, deliberate or otherwise, in its advertising at the door, such as 'Grate bargains on cheese this week' or 'Carotts – 39 cents a kilo'. I am a campaigner for Apostrophe Rights, furious when it is used for a plural and ignored for a possessive.

My favourite parts of grammar are verbs. They are strong little characters that scurry through sentences like mice through a maze, expressing action and movement. These days the trend is not to dress them up with adverbs, but to let them stand and run and jump all on their own. They are the vital, life–giving part of the language.

Prayer is a language with its own vital verbs – strong, active words that give shape and substance to how we 'do prayer'. They are words like:

- Ask
- Seek
- Knock
- Renew
- Give thanks
- Listen
- Discern
- Rest
- Journey

- Be still
- Wait
- Believe
- Confess
- Return
- Meditate
- Release
- Worship
- Forgive . . . and many more.

Over the next fortnight we are going to examine some of these vital verbs. I pray that they may be an encouragement and a blessing to you in your vital life of prayer with God.

MONDAY 11 FEBRUARY

Ask

Matthew 7:7–12

'Ask and it will be given to you . . . for everyone who asks receives'
(vv. 7,8, NIV).

Asking is basic to prayer. It's where most people begin, bringing a shopping list of requests to God, ranging from fine weather for the Sunday-school picnic, to a blessing for Aunty Mary, to help for the maths exam tomorrow. There's nothing wrong with asking, as long as that is not all our prayer becomes. Just as normal conversation is not just questions (unless you are a three-year-old!), so asking is only one part of prayer.

Jesus gave two pictures of asking in prayer which paint a backdrop for the encouragement to 'ask, seek and knock' of Matthew 7. The first is an everyday request of a child asking his father for bread or fish – basic necessities, simple requests. Would even the worst parent answer those requests maliciously, Jesus asks, and respond with a stone or a snake? The answer is 'Of course not!' So God, who is so much better than the very best parent, will give what the child asks for. Simple request – sure response.

The other picture is of a woman, a wiry persistent widow, who has to pitch her skill against a hard-as-nails judge (*Luke 18:1–8*). She pesters and bothers him until he finally relents and she gets what she wants. The illustration raises a rather puzzling question. Is God like that judge, brutal and unyielding, who only gives in to get her off his back? Repeated request – reluctant response?

If our praying is always like the second story and never like the first, we would all soon give up. But Jesus did tell that second story to encourage his disciples to keep on praying and not give up (see *Luke 18:1*). Maybe the mixture of the two is how it is for most pray-ers. Sometimes God seems to answer almost before we ask. At other times, we need to keep on bringing our requests before God and awaiting his timing for the answer.

To reflect on
Jesus gives us an envelope to wrap our prayers in – 'You may ask me for anything in my name, and I will do it' (John 14:14).

TUESDAY 12 FEBRUARY

Renew

Psalm 98

'Sing to the LORD a new song, for he has done marvellous things;
his right hand and his holy arm have worked salvation for him'
(v. I, NIV).

There are advantages in living in the southern hemisphere – such as having Christmas holidays at the beach. But there is one time of the year when I envy those who live in the northern hemisphere – Easter. For those of us 'down under', Easter comes as we head into winter, with trees letting go their leaves, late-summer colours disappearing from the gardens and the days getting cool. But in the northern hemisphere, there are signs of new life and growth all around – crocuses pushing their heads up through the snow, blossoms bursting out on wintered trees, daffodils and tulips coming to life after a long hibernation. Easter speaks a springtime language in which a vital verb is 'renew'.

The days of preparation for Easter are called Lent, from the Anglo–Saxon word for 'spring'. Lent is God's springtime, a time of spiritual renewal and growth that parallels what is happening in the world of nature. Today is called Shrove Tuesday or Mardi Gras ('Fat Tuesday') and is the beginning of the season of Lent. Over the centuries, Christians took their faith so seriously that they spent much of Lent fasting, abstaining from meat, eggs, dairy products or certain other foods. In preparation, housewives would clear out their cupboards on this day and make pancakes from the ingredients, celebrating the day with pancake tossing, pancake races and pancake parties.

Even more significant, Shrove Tuesday is the day when people interested in finding out more about the Christian faith, or joining a church, would begin their preparation classes. Each day during the weeks leading up to Easter, these inquirers would receive Bible instruction and personal prayer ministry so that, by Easter Sunday, they were ready to make their promises to God and be welcomed publicly into the Church. For mature Christians, Shrove Tuesday would be a day for reviewing one's life and commitment to Christ, and embarking on a journey of renewal.

May this day be significant for you as we begin our journey towards Easter.

*'Let him Easter in us, be a day-spring
to the dimness of us . . .'*
Gerard Manley Hopkins

WEDNESDAY 13 FEBRUARY
Return

Joel 2:12–17

'Rend your heart and not your garments. Return to the LORD your God, for he is gracious and compassionate, slow to anger and abounding in love . . .' (v. 13, NIV).

In the church calendar, Ash Wednesday is the first day of Lent. To commemorate the beginning of this significant season, many churches will hold a service of holy communion today. During the service, worshippers will have the sign of the cross traced on their forehead with ashes made from the burning of last year's Palm Sunday crosses. That is why the day is known as Ash Wednesday.

It is a day of returning and homecoming. From the earliest pages of the Old Testament and right through the Scripture, we read of the call of God to his people, 'Turn back, come home.' It is a call to relationship with himself. On this Ash Wednesday we hear that call once again. 'Return to me with all your heart.' It is a call to a drifting, distracted, wandering people to take stock and to turn our hearts towards home. The Old Testament prophet Joel's words of a God who is gracious and compassionate are echoed in the New Testament story of the prodigal son (see *Luke 15:11–24*).

This young man had demanded his family inheritance, left home and lived as though his father was already dead. His high life of freedom and friends came to a sudden stop, however, when his money ran out. Spurred on by hunger pangs, he returned home, rehearsing the speech he would give to his father. But instead of finding an angry father waiting to punish him for his wastefulness, he found his father open-armed and welcoming, having long been watching the roadway, waiting for the first sign of the boy's return. The surprised young man found himself lavished with love and generous symbols of welcome.

Jesus tells the story simply, unforgettably, to demonstrate that God is a Father just like that. He is not distant, stern or unapproachable. He loves us so much that he even places within us the longing to return to him. Then he waits patiently for us to respond to his love. 'Come home,' he calls to us again.

Let turning and returning be the focus of your prayer today.

47

THURSDAY 14 FEBRUARY
Seek

Matthew 7:7–8

'Ask and it will be given to you; seek and you will find; knock and the door will be opened to you' (v. 7, NIV).

My grandchildren love playing hide and seek. They can hardly contain the excitement of hiding (in such obvious places!) and the suspense of being found. I add to the tension, of course, by looking in un-obvious places, like behind cushions and under pot plants! I've long since realised that the real delight in the game is not in the hiding, but in the being found! It's a child's game but, like many childlike things, it gives us a glimpse of God as well. I think that he too finds pleasure in being found. Meister Eckhart said, 'God is like a person who clears his throat while hiding and so gives himself away.'

The prophet Isaiah proclaimed, 'Truly you are a God who hides himself' (Isa 45:15). His ways are a mystery. One day he seems so present and another day oh-so absent. At one stage of our lives he is like Francis Thompson's Hound of Heaven in full pursuit, calling, challenging, leading us. We can hardly keep up. But just when we think we have the God-thing all sorted out, everything suddenly changes and he seems a long way away. 'Why does he do that?' we wonder. 'Did I say something in prayer that offended him?'

The prophet Isaiah also proclaimed that the God of the Bible 'longs to be gracious to you; he rises to show you compassion' (Isa 30:18). Out of that very compassion, he calls us to seek him, to be active in our looking and searching for him.

Author Philip Yancey in *Reaching for the Invisible God* describes an exhibit of animal camouflage in a natural history museum. At first glance he saw simple scenes of summer and winter foliage. But as he stared intently at the display he noticed animals, birds and insects hidden in the foliage. So it is with God who fills this world with grace and love in all kinds of camouflage gear. The more we look, the more we will see; the more we seek, the more we will find!

'We could not seek God unless he had already found us.'

Pascal

FRIDAY 15 FEBRUARY

Rest

Matthew 11:25–30

'Come to me. Get away with me and you'll recover your life.
I'll show you how to take a real rest . . . Learn the unforced rhythms
of grace' (vv. 28,29, *The Message*).

My one and only attempt at water-skiing is still remembered with mirth by my family. 'Let go of the rope,' they yelled as I toppled off the skis and torpedoed through the water. When I finally did let go, I lay back in the water and waited for the boat to circle round and haul me aboard. Buoyed up by my life-jacket, I could sense the dark, unfathomable depths of the lake beneath me. It was a most profound moment of resting and trusting. I was reminded of the verse from Deuteronomy: 'The eternal God is your refuge, and underneath are the everlasting arms' (33:27).

Those words were but one of the promises to the children of Israel who had been brought out of Egypt by a wonder-working God. In spite of the everlasting arms that bore them up, however, they were unable to trust, unable to rest the whole weight of their circumstances on God. They rebelled, causing God to say, as much in sadness as in anger, 'They shall never enter my rest' (see *Ps 95:11; Heb 4:3*).

Resting is a significant part of praying. The literal translation for 'pray always' is 'come to rest'. This place of rest is not just a passive resignation, but an attitude of stillness and quiet alertness. Eugene Peterson says that prayer is 'in the middle voice' where we both take action and receive the action of Another. There comes a point in our praying when, having laid the burden of our heart before God, we then simply need to leave it there, resting it and ourselves in his hands. How many prodigal sons and daughters around the world are rested daily into those hands by parents who can do nothing but pray and then rest them there. The everlasting arms are always stretched out underneath us like a great supportive life-jacket. The place of prayer is the place of rest.

'Rest. Rest. Rest in God's love. The only work you are required now to do is to give your most intense attention to his still, small voice within.'

Madame Guyon

SATURDAY 16 FEBRUARY
Confess

1 John 1:5–10

'If we confess our sins, he is faithful and just and will forgive us our sins and purify us from all unrighteousness' (v. 9, NIV).

On the farm where I grew up, my father's route to the meal table was always via the 'washhouse'. He would leave his gumboots out on the back doorstep, then scrub up before coming into the kitchen. To wear muddy gumboots or come with unwashed hands into my mother's domain was simply unthinkable!

I recall my father's habit whenever I attend an Anglican service. Early on there is a time for confession, time to take off muddy gumboots, as it were, and scrub up before coming to the meal table that God has spread. I value the reminder that, in preparing to come into God's presence, I need to deal with the sin that, in Paul's words, 'so easily entangles' (*Heb 12:1*). How easy it is to hurry into a Sunday service, still buttoning a child's shirt, still red-faced about the rush to leave home or a heated exchange on the way. How easy to come to prayer with hidden sins clinging to us like mud on our boots.

Confession opens the way for us to come into God's presence. Confession sets us free from guilt and

gives us a caution about repeating that same sin in the future. But it is a process and it takes time. The first step is to place ourselves into God's hands and ask for his help. Second, we need to reflect on our thoughts, words and actions, and to acknowledge that we have sinned. Third, we need to ask God to help us see our sin through the eyes of the one we have sinned against, and also through God's eyes. Fourth, we need to examine the motives ('Why did I do that?') and the consequences ('What happened as a result?') of our sin. Fifth, we need to make a promise that, with God's help, we will change. A little man up a sycamore tree gives us a great example of that (see *Luke 19:8*). Finally, with open hands, we will be ready to receive the grace of God.

Take time to confess as you come to God in prayer today.

SUNDAY 17 FEBRUARY
Taste and See

Psalm 34

'Taste and see that the LORD is good; blessed is the man who
takes refuge in him' (v. 8, NIV).

A large multinational food corpora-
tion has in recent years discovered
a gold mine in the taste buds of
New Zealand's television viewers.
In a one-minute slot before the six
o'clock news, a vivacious young
woman, dressed in colours that
coordinate with the food she is
demonstrating, shows how easy it
is to prepare a wholesome meal. It
is compelling viewing, quick and
colourful and, at that time of day,
guaranteed to get the saliva glands
working overtime. You can almost
taste it!

The psalmist had no television
trappings, but he had an audience,
a lesson and an invitation that is
even more compelling than turkey
drumsticks in apricot sauce. 'Taste
and see,' he says, 'that the LORD is
good.' His audience are the saints
(v. 9) whom he calls 'my children',
in the style of the Hebrew wisdom
teachers. These are the students or
pupils to whom he wants to teach
the most basic of all issues – the
meaning of human life. The fear of
the Lord, he says, is the key. If you
fear the Lord, speak with integrity
and pursue peace, then God will
watch over you, especially in difficult times. You will find all your
needs met in him. This will be in
contrast to lions who, for all their
strength, still grow weak with
hunger.

The psalmist is qualified to teach
such a lesson. He gives his own
testimony to God's gracious deliverance. Whether it was from a
severe illness or a military crisis
that he was saved, he experienced
the protection of God's angels.
Having known God's deliverance
at first hand, he invites others to
'taste and see' for themselves how
trustworthy God is to those who
take refuge in him. The fear of the
Lord is not a guarantee that life
will always be easy, but it is a
guarantee that God will always be
present.

To reflect on
*Psalm 34 is traditionally associated
with the Lord's Supper, because of the
word 'taste'. The good news of God's
gracious provision for life has only one
proper response – gratitude –
Eucharist!*

MONDAY 18 FEBRUARY

Believe

Hebrews 11:1–6

'Without faith it is impossible to please God, because anyone who comes to him must believe that he exists and that he rewards those who earnestly seek him' (v. 6, NIV).

It sounds simple. 'If you pray, you need to believe that God is real.' It's like stating the obvious, but if the writer to the Hebrews felt it was worth saying, then it's worth saying again. 'Without faith it is impossible to please God, because anyone who comes to him must believe that he exists and that he rewards those who earnestly seek him.' All the verses that surround this one in what is called the 'faith chapter' of the Bible give examples of people who believed that God exists. It's a 'Who's Who' roll-call of faith – from Abel to Samuel and dozens in between. Take a look for a moment at the things these people received because of their belief – the Red Sea drying up, the walls of Jericho collapsing, escape from lions and fires, strength to endure persecution and imprisonment, victory in battle. These were heroes of the faith, big people praying big prayers to a big God.

If they could be interviewed, however, they would no doubt say that there was nothing great or special about themselves. Many of the Bible characters had rather chequered careers. Think of David, 'man after God's own heart', who was also an adulterer and murderer. Samson had physical strength but moral weakness. Gideon was hiding in fear of the Midianites when God's angel found him. These people, for all their great exploits, were people 'fraught and frayed' just like us. Their great prayers were often just, 'Help me, God!'

The important thing that these heroes of the faith held in common, however, was their belief in a great God, a prayer-answering God who could act, rescue, save, deliver, answer. On that certainty they rested the whole weight of their desperate need. Believers today are invited to do the same.

To reflect on

Prayer to God is not sending a request to Santa Claus,

It is not asking a stranger for a favour,

It is not writing a letter 'to whom it may concern',

It is bringing our request to someone who has laid down his life for us.

TUESDAY 19 FEBRUARY

Discern

Genesis 28:10–19

'Early the next morning Jacob took the stone he had placed under his head and set it up as a pillar and poured oil on top of it' (v. 18, NIV).

Discernment is where prayer and action meet. When we listen to the voice of God, we receive his guidance. While we would long for that guidance to be spoken clearly and unmistakably, one syllable at a time, most Christians do not hear the voice of God audibly. Rather, it is heard and recognised in certain movements of the heart and mind, not unlike the way we learn to recognise the voice of a parent. George Fox wrote in his journal about the Lord 'opening' a truth to him. John Calvin spoke of the 'inner testimony' of the Holy Spirit. St Ignatius talked of 'movements' of the soul.

In my own life I have often been 'nudged' to call someone or to send a note or make a visit at a particular time, not always convenient, I might add! I have been amazed at how often it seemed exactly the right time to make contact. 'How did you know that I was facing . . . ?' 'How did you know that today is the anniversary of . . . ?' Well, the fact is, I didn't know, but God did.

In George Bernard Shaw's play *St Joan*, one of the characters asks Joan of Arc why the voice of God never speaks to him the way she claims it speaks to her. 'The voice speaks to you all the time,' she says, 'but you just fail to listen.' Someone has called this 'spiritual mindlessness'. It was what Jacob suffered from at Bethel. Guided only by his own guile, he never listened to God. But one night as Jacob lay sleeping, God spoke to him in a dream and Jacob was shaken. He built an altar there, saying, 'Surely the LORD is in this place, and I was not aware of it' (*v. 16*).

As we learn to listen deeply to the voice of God and to be sensitive to his presence and promptings, we too will find ourselves building altars. 'That verse, that person, that event . . . is where God spoke to me, and I listened!'

'Discernment – a gentle receptiveness to divine breathings.'

Thomas Kelly

WEDNESDAY 20 FEBRUARY

Listen

John 10:1–16

'I am the good shepherd; I know my sheep and my sheep know me . . . They too will listen to my voice' (vv. 14,16, NIV).

I am grateful to a colleague who one day asked me to listen to her. 'I don't want advice,' she said. 'You don't need to say anything. I just want you to listen.' Over the next few months as we met together, I learned that there is more than one way to listen. There's surface listening where I simply hear the words that are spoken and then there's the deep listening of the heart – listening 'with the third ear' as it has been called. My friend taught me to listen like that, so that when the day came that God asked me to really listen to him, I was ready. For a long time my prayer had been a monologue with me doing all the talking. It seems so obvious and simple now, but it was quite a revelation to discover that prayer is really a dialogue and that there are times when I need to let God have a turn!

Jesus lived a listening life. He frequently slipped away from the crowds to be alone with God. He needed to hear the deeper sounds of God's voice, away from the constant clamour of people's demands. He spoke with confidence that those who followed him would hear and recognise his voice. He used the familiar figure of the shepherd as illustration. Separate flocks of sheep would often be sheltered together at night in the land of Palestine. In the morning each shepherd, with his distinctive sing–song voice, would call his sheep out and the sheep would respond. It was a voice they knew. It was a voice they had learned to trust from long days – sometimes years – of following the shepherd to fresh pasture and safe watering holes. Jesus said, 'I'm like that. I'm the good shepherd who protects you. I lay down my life for the sheep. Listen to my voice and I'll keep you safe and lead you to nourishing pasture.'

Today as you come to prayer, don't say anything. Simply put yourself into a listening pose, be attentive to God and ask him to speak to you.

THURSDAY 21 FEBRUARY
Be Still

I Kings 19:9–13

'After the earthquake came a fire, but the LORD was not in the fire. And after the fire came a gentle whisper' (v. 12, NIV).

For the deep listening of the heart to happen in prayer, the sounds of the outer world need to be hushed. It is difficult, if not impossible, to listen to God when we are bombarded by a constant cacophony of noise, from intrusive conversation on the train, to blaring TV in the lounge, to piped music in the shopping mall. Many people today find that they just have to 'get away from it all' in order to be still and listen.

One man who took 'getting away from it all' to an extreme was Paul Hawker, an Australian film maker. Although successful in his work and secure in his family relationships, Hawker reached midlife feeling restless and rudderless. He described himself as 'alone, hollow and a fraud' and he needed to find God and himself again. He bought the necessary mountain equipment and enough food to last for forty days and set out alone to the treacherous Tararua Mountain Range in New Zealand. His book *Soul Survivor* tells the story of those forty days of solitude.

He endured snow storms and bitter winter conditions when gale-force winds of sub-zero tempera-tures blew for days on end, making him wonder what he was doing there. But there were also moments of overwhelming beauty and sheer ecstasy when he clearly heard the voice of God. That voice, often challenging, always companionable, brought him back to himself and to the love of God.

Another day, on another mountain, the prophet Elijah stood listening. Feeling alone, pursued, abandoned, he heard the voice of God, not in the destructive wind or earthquake or fire, but in a gentle whisper. Our first step into prayer today may be to find a quiet, still place where we too can listen for that gentle sound.

'My soul journey didn't start and end on the mountain. It's been ongoing for years and is still going on. But up there, uncluttered by events, other people, and with my defenses down, God stood revealed in ways I'd never experienced before . . . On the mountain I found my true home.'

Paul Hawker

FRIDAY 22 FEBRUARY
Wait

Isaiah 40:27–31

'Those who wait for the LORD shall renew their strength, they shall mount up with wings like eagles, they shall run and not be weary, they shall walk and not faint' (v. 31, NRSV).

We live in a waiting world. All around us, it seems, there are people waiting. A child waits for a birthday, a young woman waits for marriage, a couple waits for a baby, a frail elderly person waits to die. Every day we wait, in supermarket queues, at traffic lights, in doctors' waiting rooms. As life around us gets faster and busier, in this '24/7 era' as it is called, waiting seems to become more common and increasingly frustrating.

When it comes to prayer, waiting is part of the package. From the psalmist ('Be still before the LORD and wait patiently for him' [Ps 37:7]), to Jesus ('Wait for the gift my Father promised' [Acts 1:4]), to Paul ('Wait for the blessed hope' [Tit 2:13]), we are encouraged over and over again to 'wait for the Lord'. Waiting has been described as 'the hardest work of hope'. So often we wait for a 'not yet' that feels like a 'not ever'. But the waiting is essential, for God's work of forming character within us as we wait is even more important than what we actually wait for.

Sue Monk Kidd, in *When the Heart Waits*, describes watching a monk who was sitting perfectly still under a tree. He was a picture of waiting and she asked him later how he could just sit there, doing nothing. He replied, 'When you're waiting, you're not doing nothing. You're doing the most important thing there is. You're allowing your soul to grow up. If you can't be still and wait, you can't become what God created you to be.'

Henri Nouwen describes the unique relationship between trapeze artists on the high wires of the circus. The flyer who lets go of the bar and arcs out into the air must not make any attempt to catch the catcher. He must simply trust the catcher and wait to be caught. Whatever you wait for in prayer today, trust the strong arms of God to catch you at his precise moment.

'Dios tarda pero no olvida –
God delays but he does not forget.'
(Spanish proverb)

SATURDAY 23 FEBRUARY
Give Thanks

Luke 17:11–19

'One of them, when he saw he was healed, came back, praising God in a loud voice . . . and thanked him' (vv. 15,16, NIV).

When our children were young, we taught them to pray by saying 'thank you'. 'Thank you, God, for a sunny day.' 'Thank you for my favourite toy.' The beginnings of prayer were as basic and simple as that, within the reach of even a two–year–old. Somewhere along the way as we grow in prayer, the shopping–list approach seems to take over. 'Lord, there are so many things up ahead of me today and I need your help with . . . and . . . I'll come back later and thank you.'

Stand by a dusty road for a moment with ten men carrying the stigma of leprosy. Socially ostracised because of their disease, they held themselves at a distance and called out to Jesus for pity. He responded with compassion, then told them to go and get checked out by the priests. Luke says, 'As they went, they were cleansed.' But one stopped, came back, threw himself at Jesus' feet and thanked him. Personal contact, heartfelt thanks. Is it stretching the story to say that the others were cleansed, but this man was healed at an even deeper level? 'Your faith has made you well,' said Jesus. 'You're no longer diseased. You don't even have to think like a leprosy sufferer any more.' The words 'thank you' somehow made a difference for this man.

Jesus' life of prayer has been described as marked by 'wild gratitude'. Wild in its flights of exultation and wild in its fierce constancy in all seasons of life. He lived a daily, gratitude–filled experience of the goodness of God and his world. 'Look at the birds!' 'Look at the wild flowers!' He knew the poetry of lament but he never forgot the poetry of praise, even in the most difficult circumstances. Developing the poetry of praise, a thankful spirit towards God and towards others, can open our eyes to the overwhelming goodness of God all around us. Let us, like Jesus, be people of 'wild gratitude'.

To reflect on
'If the only prayer you say in your whole life is "thank you" that will suffice.'
Meister Eckhart

SUNDAY 24 FEBRUARY
Deliver Us from Evil

Psalm 35

'Contend, O LORD, with those who contend with me; fight against those who fight against me' (v. 1, NIV).

Psalm 35 is a desperate prayer for help. The psalmist's circumstances are unclear, but the legal language of the psalm – 'contend', 'vindicate', 'rise to my defence' – suggests that it could be the prayer of a person who has been falsely accused. However, the legal language mixes and mingles with military terms – 'fight', 'shield', 'spear' – suggesting that it could be the prayer of a king for God's help in dealing with the nation's enemies. So whether this is a personal prayer or the heart cry of one on behalf of the whole nation, strugglers and sufferers can find here a resource for prayer and help.

'Contend with them, Lord,' the psalmist cries, 'take up shield, brandish spear and javelin.' He is asking God to take charge of a situation that is beyond his control. While God acts on his behalf, the psalmist determines to trust and rejoice in him. He knows that suffering is not a sign of God's disfavour, but an opportunity to see God at work. His enemies, however, are like Job's friends, interpreting suffering as evidence of sinfulness. Their ruthless questioning leaves the psalmist forlorn. This word is often associated with the sadness of childlessness, so it is a word of relationship, which fittingly describes how he responded when others were suffering. With sackcloth and fasting, he showed the usual signs of mourning that a family member would show. But that was met with slander and malice from them when he was in trouble. Like wild animals they mocked him and gnashed their teeth. He now calls on God to come to his defence and to establish justice for him.

Psalm 35 is the prayer of Elijah or Jeremiah or Job or Jesus, all of whom were mocked without cause, all of whom suffered on account of their righteousness and faithfulness to God. For modern-day followers who suffer while others scorn, and trust while others taunt, this psalm offers a pattern of prayer to a God who delights in the wellbeing (*shalom*) of his servants.

A prayer for today
Thy will be done . . . deliver us from evil.

A QUESTION OF ETHICS
Introduction

Dr James Read is the Executive Director of the Salvation Army's Ethics Centre in Winnipeg, Canada. The mission of the Centre is to provide ethics consultation, research and educational services informed by a Salvationist Christian perspective. He writes:

Ethics, according to the dictionary, is 'the science of moral value'. By this it means that ethics involves a careful examination of what behaviour is right and wrong; what we have a right to do and what we are obligated not to do; what makes a person virtuous and what corrupts character. Ethics tries to identify the principles that make it right to do something, not only on this occasion, but also in general. And if those principles can be rank-ordered, it tries to organise them so that we see which values are most important of all. Understanding moral value is not enough, however. Ethics is also concerned with motivating people to do what is right and to do it for the right reasons. Christian ethics is the effort to do all of this in light of the person, teaching and example of Jesus Christ.

It would be impossible to cover all of Christian ethics in a couple of weeks of devotional study, so we will focus on a selection of the prominent ethical issues that come up in the Gospels – love, power, money, sex, time, etc. Ethical reflection often begins with a question, 'What ought I to do in this difficult situation?' or 'Why should I do that?' We will reflect on six questions that people asked Jesus, and then six questions Jesus himself asked.

Sometimes questions were directed at Jesus in order to humiliate or trap him. But seriously posed or not, Jesus made the question a means by which to uncover gospel values. Some who came to scoff may stay to listen.

My hope is that these devotionals will help all readers love God more fully with mind and soul and strength, and love people as Christ has loved them.

MONDAY 25 FEBRUARY
The Greatest Commandment

Matthew 22:34–40

'Teacher, which is the greatest commandment in the Law?'
(v. 36, NIV).

Matthew says that the Pharisee who posed this question did so to 'test' Jesus. Shortly beforehand, Jesus had been approached by Sadducees who tried to trip him up on questions about the afterlife. In that instance Jesus had amazed the crowds with his ability to outsmart his opponents. It may be that the Pharisees are now taking their turn at trying to embarrass Jesus.

But the question need not spring from dishonest motives. In Mark's account of this encounter, the Pharisee lawyer seems to be genuinely struggling with the question. According to the Pharisees, there were 613 written commandments that God gave through Moses. In addition, the rabbis said there were innumerable 'interpretations' of these commandments. There were, for example, thirty-nine types of labour prohibited on the Sabbath, including writing two letters of the alphabet! Anyone who took these laws seriously would need a way of rank-ordering them to know what to do when they conflicted. (*Mark 12:32–33* shows that the lawyer saw how the

priority of love resolved a potential dilemma.)

Our ethical dilemmas are different from those of the Pharisees who lived in Jesus' day, but we still face them. And in those times, we ourselves may want to ask, 'Jesus, which is the most important value?'

Jesus' answer is that the love of God (*Deut 6:5*) and love of neighbour (*Lev 19:18*) are so important that the entire Law and Prophets hang on them (*v. 40*). The apostle Paul offered the same answer when he said, 'The only thing that counts is faith expressing itself through love' (*Gal 5:6*).

This does not mean that it is unimportant for Christians to talk about financial ethics or sexual ethics or political ethics. But it does mean that when we are talking about these other issues we should not lose sight of the deeper values that undergird our ethical principles. As Jesus would have it, he wants us to discover how the love of God and love of neighbour connect with what we should say about poverty and homosexuality and oppression and the rest.

TUESDAY 26 FEBRUARY
Who Is My Neighbour?

Luke 10:25–37

'[An expert in the law] wanted to justify himself, so he asked Jesus, "And who is my neighbour?" ' (v. 29, NIV).

The story of the Good Samaritan is one of the best-known stories in all the Bible, and is rightly regarded as one of the key teachings in Christian ethics. Jesus tells that story in answer to the question in our text.

We are told that the lawyer wanted to 'justify' himself. Does this mean that he wants a rejoinder that will save face? Jesus had easily parried his first question and made him look rather silly. Maybe he's asking a second question to cover his embarrassment. Or perhaps he is sincere and wants to know whom it would be ethical to exclude. The question of where a person ought to draw the boundaries of his care was a serious question among the Pharisees. The natural reading of Leviticus 19:18 is that the Jew is to count other Jews as neighbours. But Sirach 12:4 says not to help a sinner. Have Jews who flout the law lost the right to be neighbours? Leviticus 19:34 says to love the resident alien. Does this include the Roman occupation forces?

Whatever the questioner's motivation, Jesus' story shows us that 'neighbour' is to apply without boundaries, that 'neighbour' is to be defined by our common humanity – not by nationality, occupation, or character.

While we might be tempted to be critical of the lawyer for being so 'thick', we need to ask how often we have 'crossed to the other side of the road'. Do our actions show that we have drawn a line separating those we are prepared to care about from those we are prepared to ignore? Do we catch ourselves justifying a narrow definition of neighbour?

One last observation. Many believe that Jesus intended the lawyer to identify himself as one of the story's characters – specifically, the man lying by the roadside. If he did that (and if we do that) the question of who is my neighbour becomes not 'who must I help?' but 'who will be willing to help me?' And what a transforming experience it is to be helped by someone we would have ignored or patronised!

WEDNESDAY 27 FEBRUARY
A Question of Money

John 12:1–8

'But one of his disciples, Judas Iscariot, who was later to betray him, objected, "Why wasn't this perfume sold and the money given to the poor? It was worth a year's wages" ' (vv. 4,5, NIV).

We don't know much about Mary, but the cameos we get here and in Luke 10:38–42 portray her as a woman devoted to Jesus. Why she owned very expensive perfume we don't know. Jesus says it was for the day of his burial, but in saying this, he is probably talking about what God intended it for, not what Mary originally had in mind. Maybe it was her dowry, her financial security.

To pour the whole jarful over Jesus must have got the attention of everyone present. But it took Judas to say aloud what may have been going through many minds: 'What a waste! Think of the good that could have been done!' Ironically, it is Judas who comes off as the ethical one and Jesus the one who supports extravagance. But Judas' words, even if true in themselves, were emptied of moral value because he had no real interest in the poor. He not only betrayed Jesus, he betrayed the poor too (v. 6).

Unfortunately, people in generations since Judas have twisted Jesus' words, 'You will always have the poor among you', into a justification for a lax attitude towards poverty and economic imbalance. We know Jesus did not endorse that!

Can we generalise Mary's behaviour? Is it to teach us any lesson about how we ought to live life in general, or is it appropriate only because of Jesus' unique status? Christian tradition has held Mary up as an example (*Mark* 14:9) for her rejection of the utilitarian ethic, her rejection of the ethics that says what's right is right because it generates the greatest good.

Sometimes what Christian ethics calls for is an extravagant gesture of love. Teresa of Calcutta is a modern–day heroine precisely because the dying children for whom she poured out her life were not a good 'investment', but she saw they deserved love all the same. There will always be those rational–sounding voices critical of her impracticality, but one look into the face of the emaciated child cradled in loving arms renders those voices hollow.

THURSDAY 28 FEBRUARY
A Question of Marriage

Mark 10:1–12

'Some Pharisees came and tested him by asking, "Is it lawful for a man to divorce his wife?" ' (v. 2, NIV).

Why, we should wonder, do the Pharisees ask this question? How do they figure this will trip Jesus up? In Matthew's account of the incident (*Matt 19:3*), Jesus is asked whether a man may divorce his wife 'for any cause'. This puts the question in the context of a debate among the rabbis. Some interpreted Deuteronomy 24 as permitting a man to end the marriage if his wife burnt the toast. Others taught that divorce was permissible only for serious breaches of the marriage, such as an affair.

Mark's starker way of reporting the question allows Jesus' reply to stand out more sharply: 'What did Moses command?' Well, obviously Moses never commanded anyone to divorce. By asking this question Jesus forces the Pharisees away from the tendency to focus on how to deal with the breakdown of marriage, to adjudicate which divorces are justified, which are excusable and which are plain wrong. Jesus wants those who are testing him to concentrate first on what *marriage* is about, and what is good about marriage.

If marriage was tenuous in Jesus' day, it is even more so today. Before we get into any discussion of what is permissible when a marriage is beyond repair, Jesus would direct us to examine what Christian marriage itself is and is not. It is not a mere contract cut to the couple's terms and entered into for enhancement of self-interest. Marriage is part of God's creation design. It is to be covenantal, and it is to transform the man and woman so profoundly that their interests are not two but one. In Ephesians 5:32 Paul tells us it is God's intention that marriage be an earthly comparison of the mystical union of Christ and the Church.

Long before we get to questions about the ethics of divorce, those of us who are married need to ask ourselves whether we understand and live up to what God did design and command. And all of us, married or single, need to ask whether our church and our society can be made more congenial to marriage along God's lines.

FRIDAY 1 MARCH
A Question of Power

John 19:1–12

' "Do you refuse to speak to me?" Pilate said. "Don't you realise I have power either to free you or to crucify you?" ' (v. 10, NIV).

John's Gospel presents the trial and crucifixion of Jesus as a power struggle between Pilate, Rome's senior representative in Palestine, and Caiaphas and the Sanhedrin, the Jewish establishment in Jerusalem. Each side is more interested in maintaining the upper hand than in seeing that justice is done. When the charge against Jesus is changed from sedition to blasphemy (v. 7), Pilate opens a new investigation. And he uses his typical power–game strategy, 'Answer me, or I'll crucify you!'

Unintimidated, Jesus replies, 'You would have no power over me if it were not given to you from above.' This seems to unsettle Pilate. 'From then on, Pilate tried to set Jesus free' (v. 12). He is all too aware that he holds his position only at Caesar's pleasure. (In AD 31 Aelius Sejanus, Pilate's patron in Rome, fell out of favour with the Emperor Tiberius and was killed.) Pilate had asked where Jesus came from. When Jesus replied to his threat unperturbed, Pilate may have wondered if Jesus had inside connections with Rome.

But all that is at the human level. Jesus actually intends to draw our attention to the fact that all human power and authority ultimately derives from God. In truth, neither Caiaphas nor Pilate nor Caesar is in control – God is (see *Acts 4:27–28*).

Elsewhere Scripture enjoins us to pray for those in positions of authority. This is because justice cannot exist without social structures (*1 Tim 2:2*). It is also because people who are in positions of authority are routinely tempted to wield power rather than administer justice. They therefore need Christians to pray that they will be brought up short, as Pilate was by Jesus, when that temptation rears its head.

Scripture also enjoins us to pray for those who, like Jesus before Pilate, are being denied justice. Around the world today there are tyrants who have no place for ethics, and they need to be countered by Christians who will 'remember those in prison as if [they] were their fellow-prisoners, and those who are ill-treated as if [they themselves] were suffering' (*Heb 13:3*).

SATURDAY 2 MARCH
A Question of the Sabbath

Mark 2:23–28

'The Pharisees said to him, "Look, why are they doing what is unlawful on the Sabbath?"' (v. 24, NIV).

Jesus had been walking through a field with his disciples on a Sabbath during harvest season. The disciples picked and ate some of the grain.

To us this might seem innocent enough, but to the Pharisees what happened was a scandal. The fourth commandment stipulated that the Sabbath was to be kept free from work. According to the Pharisees, the disciples had violated this by harvesting and threshing (Luke 6:1 says they rubbed the grain between their hands). The question they put to Jesus was really a demand that he chastise his followers for their wrongdoing.

Jesus didn't do this, however. Instead he offered two different 'defences' to the Pharisees. He referred to David and his men eating the consecrated bread (vv. 25,26) to remind the Pharisees that even their own ethical system didn't make a work-free Sabbath the highest value. The rabbis said, 'He who saves a life saves the whole world.' Doctors ought to attend to emergencies seven days a week.

But, the Pharisees might object, the disciples weren't starving, they were snacking! Which brings us to Jesus' second response: 'Sabbath was made for man, not man for the Sabbath.' In Jesus' eyes, the fact that his disciples were merely enjoying a snack illustrates what Sabbath is really about. It's about allowing human existence to rise above the task-orientation of the workplace that commands so much of our attention so much of the time.

The Ten Commandments (Exod 20) open with God's reminder that he has taken the Hebrew people out of slavery. Sabbath is to be a regular celebration of their freedom and of their liberator. If the overly conscientious Pharisees needed to be reminded of this, so do we. However Sabbath gets woven into our lives (and to insist that it be Saturday or Sunday becomes another legalism), it will be refreshing to cease 'from the need to accomplish and be productive, from the worry and tension that accompany our modern criterion of efficiency... and from the humdrum and meaninglessness that result when life is pursued without the Lord at the centre of it all' (Marva Dawn).

SUNDAY 3 MARCH

The Fountain of Life

Psalm 36

'For with you is the fountain of life; in your light we see light'
(v. 9, NIV).

David, named as the servant of the Lord, begins Psalm 36 by writing about the wicked who are servants of themselves. His description of the wicked is like a modern computer-generated identikit picture such as the police use to identify criminals. In the area of speech, the wicked are deceitful. When it comes to action, they show no evidence of wisdom or goodness. As far as thinking is concerned, they are arrogantly fearless of God, full of self-flattery, proud of their sin, devising mischief even when in bed. The wicked are the very embodiment of evil as they pursue their own selfish ways in total dedication.

The psalmist has no doubt about the reality of the wicked, but he knows too a far deeper and more enduring reality. He lifts his heart in praise to God and in two verses describes, as in an identikit picture, the character of God – his steadfast, unfailing love, his faithfulness, his righteousness and his justice. In a great sweep of language he describes each attribute of God in cosmic terms that are arranged from highest to lowest – the heavens above all, the skies above the earth, the mighty mountains as the highest point of earth and the great deep below the earth. In other words, God's character is built into the very structure of the universe. Everyone and everything, both man and beast, depends on God for its very existence. To take refuge in God is simply to acknowledge that dependence.

This is precisely the opposite of what the wicked do as they assert their own self-sufficiency. In words reminiscent of Psalm 1, he affirms that the way of the wicked will in the end prove futile. For the righteous, however, God continues to give an abundant provision of all that is needed. Life is not a reward to be earned, but a gift to be received. Light and life, shown supremely in the person of Jesus (John 1:4), are offered still today to all who will receive.

Prayer
Lord, let your light shine on me and your life live through me today.

MONDAY 4 MARCH
The Golden Rule

Luke 6:27–36

'If you love those who love you, what credit is that to you? Even "sinners" love those who love them. And if you do good to those who are good to you, what credit is that to you? Even "sinners" do that' (vv. 32, 33, NIV).

Perhaps the most basic principle in ethics is the Golden Rule – 'Do to others as you would have them do to you' (v. 31). In some sense it's supposed to be *obviously* true, the kind of thing we learn at our mother's knee. But when Jesus immediately follows up his statement of the Golden Rule with the two questions (vv. 32,33), he makes us see that what seems obvious in one light isn't at all the way we live much of our lives.

So much of life is not lived according to a principle of how we would *want* to be treated by others, but by how we have *in fact* been treated by them. Friends are kind to friends who have been kind to them. In society, the market and the justice system are apparently based on a principle of quid pro quo.

Jesus is not saying that loving those who love us is wrong. But he's showing that it's very limiting and very conservative. And it's probably not really the way we want to be treated ourselves. Do we want our family to love us only on condition that we are ready to love them back? Wouldn't we rather have a parent who is ready to welcome us back even if we wrong them (15:20)?

Which brings us to Jesus' strong words about loving the enemy (vv. 27,33). If we hate those who hate us, what credit is that to us? Animosity fuels violence and destroys the possibility of community. How is the cycle of violence going to be broken?

Jesus says it will mean going back to what seemed obvious at our mother's knee. If we were to treat others as we ourselves want to be treated by them, not as we have in fact been treated, it would be impossible to regard them as enemies. We would be more generous. We would take more risks on people. We would be readier to show others the grace we want to receive for ourselves – and indeed have already received in Christ.

TUESDAY 5 MARCH
A Question of Doing Good

Matthew 25:31–40

'Then the righteous will answer him, "Lord, when did we see you hungry and feed you, or thirsty and give you something to drink? When did we see you a stranger and invite you in, or needing clothes and clothe you? When did we see you sick or in prison and go to visit you?" ' (vv. 37–39, NIV).

These questions come from the surprised righteous people in Jesus' story of the 'sheep' and the 'goats'. There are others – the goats – who ask different questions. 'When did we see you hungry, Lord, and *not* feed you?' (v. 44). Jesus does not suggest that 'the goats' would not have fed the Lord had they met up with him. In fact, they are the sort of people who would have been delighted by any opportunity to feed a king. 'If only we had known these were your brothers!', we can hear them complain. The problem, of course, is that their 'care' would have been contingent on the connections.

The 'righteous' in the story are commended for acting differently. The righteous were quite unchoosy about who they helped. If the need was bodily, they met it with food, drink or clothing. If the need was spiritual, they met it by offering relationship. They didn't let the strangeness of the stranger become a barrier. They didn't let fear of illness isolate the sick. They didn't forget the prisoner. Seeing a human in need they had compassion. That they were serving the brothers of a king comes as quite a surprise to them.

Bible teachers sometimes define *agape* as obedient love that springs from the will, not the affections. There is an element of this in the Bible. But the danger is that it makes an emotionless philanthropy the highest point of Christian ethics. We won't get that message from this story. This story is full of emotion. It clearly teaches that Jesus would have us loving each other with the compassion of brothers and sisters – being the family of the Lord himself.

The heart of the gospel is that God loves the world. What greater evidence could there be than the incarnation of the Son in the person of Jesus of Nazareth? The story of the sheep and the goats tells us the identification is so complete that when God finds one person who genuinely cares for another, he feels it personally and he feels it for eternity.

WEDNESDAY 6 MARCH
A Question of Gratitude

Luke 17:11–19

'Jesus asked, "Were not all ten cleansed? Where are the other nine? Was no-one found to return and give praise to God except this foreigner?" ' (v. 17, NIV).

This story tells of Jesus healing physical ailments, but it means to teach us much more than that Jesus has miraculous power over disease. The ten lepers had become outcasts. Leviticus 13 ordered lepers to live 'outside the camp' and to call out 'Unclean, unclean!' whenever anyone got close to them. We can see that those instructions were still operative in Jesus' day, since it's outside the village that he meets them. They call out to him in a loud voice (vv. 12,13), indicating that they were observing the ancient quarantine. What this means is that Jesus' miracle not only cured their bodies, but effected a social healing too, since it would now be possible for them to be reintegrated into society. An irony about all of this is that it happened as Jesus was travelling along the border country to Jerusalem where he would himself be made an outcast.

The one man who returns and gives thanks is clearly to be the example of what all ten ought to have done. We can try to make excuses for the others – they were so overcome by their good fortune,

by the sight of wife and children once again, that they understandably forgot Jesus. We can try to minimise the action of the Samaritan – did the others have further to travel to get to a priest? Making excuses for our own faults and minimising the good done by others is common when we have not done all we should, but it doesn't change the facts. All ten ex-lepers should have said thank you to Jesus.

We can draw a general observation that is very important in our times. Looking for opportunities to say thank you to God or to fellow human beings seems to have given way to a quest for opportunities to assert our rights. Now, rights-talk is not inherently anti-Christian. In fact, human rights movements are historically rooted in Christianity. But this story should remind us that Christian ethics begins with gratitude for what we have been given, not with entitlement to what we deserve.

THURSDAY 7 MARCH
A Question of Condemnation

John 8:1–11

'Jesus straightened up and asked her, "Woman, where are they? Has no-one condemned you?" ' (v. 10, NIV).

Of many interesting features in the story of the woman caught in adultery, the most interesting, ethically speaking, is Jesus' question and what follows it. 'Neither do I condemn you. Go now and leave your life of sin.'

Before we get to that, however, we find ourselves asking how this woman managed to get caught in the very act. According to Deuteronomy 19:15, accusations must be supported by the testimony of at least two eyewitnesses, and one wonders how two spies came to be in the bedroom. J. D. M. Derrett speculates that the woman's husband cynically set it up, instead of trying to regain his wife's love.

We also find ourselves wondering whether the lawyers and Pharisees are really interested in seeing the woman put to death. Or is this too a set-up, using her as the pawn in a game whose real goal is the death of Jesus? We wonder whether Jesus had a special sensitivity to women accused of adultery, since he himself was the son of a woman who could have been so accused.

We wonder what Jesus wrote on the ground. Was he simply buying time so he could contain his anger? Was he writing down the names of women with whom the accusers had had sex?

All of these are interesting issues, but they must not divert our attention from the conclusion, which is a narrative enactment of the good news announced in John 3:17. God did not send his Son into the world to condemn the world, but to save it!

Those who are committed to Jesus follow his ethics. It's not that Christians are to condone adultery, or to think adultery or any other wrongdoing a trivial matter, but rather that Christians are to seek the redemption and transformation of people who have done wrong. We Christians should remember that we all have stood in the spot where the adulterous woman stood, having done something we ought not to have done, surrounded by voices all too eager to make us pay. And we too have been released by Jesus!

FRIDAY 8 MARCH
Job Interview on the Beach

John 21:15-19

'When they had finished eating, Jesus said to Simon Peter, "Simon son of John, do you truly love me more than these?" ' (v. 15, NIV).

In one way the setting for this story is very ordinary – a group of fishermen have just finished breakfast. In another way it is quite remarkable, however, since this very ordinary encounter takes place after Jesus' resurrection, and records some of the Lord's last words to a man who had been one of his closest friends.

The traditional interpretation is that this conversation is a reinstatement of Peter after his thrice-repeated denial of Jesus (see *John 18*). We can only imagine how profoundly Peter longed for this opportunity! A long time before he had asked Jesus how many times it was necessary to forgive someone who had caused offence (*Matt 18:21*). Now he himself was the man needing forgiveness, and Jesus, true to his character, lived out his own teaching. Not only was Peter's betrayal not held forever against him, but also Jesus was prepared to entrust him with a major leadership position in the Church.

So this reinstatement was also a kind of job interview. Jesus asks, 'Peter, do you love me more than these, that is, more than you love the nets, and boats, and the other trappings of the fishing life?' When Peter says yes, Jesus follows up with, 'Feed my lambs, take care of my sheep.' In other words, 'I am giving you the job of pastoring the believers I am leaving behind.'

When you think about it, isn't 'Do you love me?' an odd question to ask in a job interview? Wouldn't we expect Peter to be asked about his education, skills and experience? These are important, surely, since the Church needs well-trained leaders. But for Jesus the non-negotiable was Peter's character.

Newspapers discuss whether people in public political leadership need to be good people or whether political savvy and a knowledge of the issues are what are really necessary. When it comes to the question of who ought to be entrusted with the leadership of his followers, Jesus is unequivocal – only someone with the requisite moral character, someone who loves God and relates to and cares for other people as God's own 'flock', will do.

SATURDAY 9 MARCH
A Question of Greatness

Mark 9:33–37

'They came to Capernaum. When he was in the house, he asked them, "What were you arguing about on the road?" ' (v. 33, NIV).

The Bible does not gloss over the flaws of Jesus' disciples. Just like us, the first disciples could be argumentative, obtuse, self-seeking. And like them, we need Jesus to question us if our flaws are to be corrected.

The position of this story in Mark's Gospel is interesting because it is sandwiched between two stories that highlight the disciples' powerlessness. In the story that precedes this, Jesus heals a boy the disciples had been unable to help. And in the story that follows, we learn of a man who has miraculous power, though he is 'not one of us'. And yet in the middle story, filled with a pride that ignores their actual ineffectiveness, the Twelve argue about which of them is greatest!

Jesus needed to instruct them as to the real measure of Christian greatness. Greatness is not how close you sit to the Master (10:37), nor a position that provides the opportunity to throw your weight around (10:42). Christian greatness is found in a person's character. It is found in the people who subordinate their own interests to the interests of others (v. 35). It is found in those who have time for children (vv. 36,37) and others who don't seem to matter (Matt 25:42,43).

The message is familiar, but why is it so hard to grasp? In the early church, parties formed around Peter and Paul and Apollos, each championing their man as best (1 Cor 1:12). Christians fought over which kind of 'gift' was greatest! 'Is it the gift of tongues? The gift of administration? Which?' To which Paul replied as Jesus had before him, 'The greatest of these is love' (1 Cor 13:13).

Pride is still a problem. Merely hearing instruction in Christian ethics is not enough. If we are to be 'great' as God would have us be great, if we are to do right as God would have us do right, there must be a transformation in our being. Fortunately, that is what God is wanting to do (Rom 5:5).

SUNDAY 10 MARCH
God Rules the World!

Psalm 37:1–11

'The salvation of the righteous comes from the LORD; he is their stronghold in time of trouble' (v. 39, NIV).

Why do bad things happen to good people? Where is God when I'm hurting? Why do unbelievers have an easier life, make more money, get away with dishonesty? Simply stated, the question of Psalm 37 is: Why does God allow evil?

The psalmist gives us no easy answers, but he does offer a perspective. He takes us by the hand, as it were, and leads us a long trek up a steep hill. From the top, our perspective of the land below is quite different from what we usually see when down in the valley. Up here, the air is crisp, the issues clear. Look at the wicked, he tells us. They plot and scheme, gnash their teeth, default on debts, use power to gain advantage. They seem to prosper and flourish. But look at what is coming to them – destruction. They have their day, but it will not be a long day! Their career is brief, as momentary as a wisp of smoke, their future non-existent. God laughs at them for he knows what is coming.

In contrast, look at the righteous, those who trust in the Lord and are humble, blameless, generous, upright, peaceable, and who speak the wisdom that comes from meditating on God's law. These are the ones who will inherit the land, who will be established and blessed with safety and peace.

The psalm is an instructional poem of wisdom that carefully weaves a contrast between the righteous and the wicked. The righteous are those who are attentive to God's instruction, the wicked those who live without any reference to God. For the moment, we are 'in the valley' as it were, where the wicked do seem to prosper and flourish. We live our lives in the present moment but also in the 'not yet' perspective of eternity. So the psalmist's strong call, 'do not fret . . . trust in the Lord . . . delight . . . commit . . . be still', is a call to rest in the providence of God.

To reflect on
We are called to live both for the future and by the future.

THE SEASON OF HOME-COMING

Introduction

The Bible is full of home-coming stories. There's Abraham, Jacob, Ruth and Naomi, Jonah and countless other pilgrims whose stories wander through the pages of the Old Testament. In the New Testament there's the gripping story of the prodigal son that Jesus told, describing a young man who turned away from his father and all that home represented. He lost everything but in the process found himself and eventually came home to a welcome beyond his imagining. T. S. Eliot wrote that each of us is 'outward bound only in order to return ... the inward way from where we started, and to see the place for the first time'.

The season of Lent leading up to Easter is the season of home-coming. It was so for Jesus. As he journeyed to Jerusalem there was a sense of 'going home'. Even though suffering and death lay ahead of him, the cross that would end his life was in reality the fulfilment of his life, the completion of his mission. The love of the Father that he had preached and taught about would be fully and for all time displayed in an open-armed gesture of love and welcome. The forgiveness that he won that day by taking the death penalty for our sins would make home-coming possible for us all.

Malcolm Muggeridge spent years resisting God's love and calling. Describing his conversion, he says he was overwhelmed by a sense of home-coming, picking up the threads of a lost life, responding to a bell which had long been ringing, taking his place at a table that had long been vacant.

As we walk this pilgrim way with Jesus, may these be days of home-coming for us as well. Like countless other prodigals, may we catch a fresh and overwhelming glimpse of the Father's love, step into his welcome home, and take our place at the table that has been vacant and waiting for us.

MONDAY 11 MARCH
The Season of Home-Coming

Psalm 23

'Surely goodness and love will follow me all the days of my life,
and I will dwell in the house of the LORD forever' (v. 6, NIV).

Easter is the season of home-coming. During the weeks of Lent leading up to Easter, we watch Jesus as he journeys towards Jerusalem. It is not a warm and relaxing home-coming that awaits him there, but an aggressive arrest, an unfair trial and a horrific death. In spite of knowing that, he moves steadily towards Jerusalem, clear-eyed and focused.

His whole life has been a preparation for this home-coming. He was born into a refugee family but by the time he was an adolescent he knew where home was. Being mistakenly left behind in Jerusalem after a trip to the city to celebrate the Feast of the Passover, he was found by his relieved parents in the temple courts. Surprised at their anxiety, he asked, 'Didn't you know I would be here, in my Father's house?' By the age of twelve he clearly knew who he was, where he belonged and what he had come to do. His mission – to turn the hearts of people back to God. In other words, to make home-coming possible for all of us.

Our home-coming journey during this Lenten period begins in the symbolism of Ash Wednesday. The ash from the burning of last year's palm crosses is rubbed into the forehead with the blessing, 'Remember that you are dust and to dust you shall return.' The dust on the forehead is a reminder of our humanity. It is the image of the commonplace, the symbol of ordinariness, of nothingness. There is always more than enough of it. But the sign on the forehead is the sign of the cross that declares that dust has been redeemed. In taking flesh, the Son of God took on our humanity. The One who made himself nothing (*Phil 2:7*) redeems our nothingness. He fills our dust with the glory and grandeur of God, takes the terror out of death, and invites us home.

To reflect on
' "Going home" is a journey to the heart of who we are, a place where we can be ourselves and welcome the reality of our beauty and our pain.'

Jean Vanier

TUESDAY 12 MARCH
Time for Unpacking

Matthew 4:1–11

'Worship the Lord your God, and serve him only' (v. 10, NIV).

Most journeys begin with packing. In our household that means collecting a suitcase from the garage and tossing items into it over several days before the start of the journey. The journey of faith that we take during the season of Lent, however, begins not with packing, but with unpacking. This is a journey of the heart. There is no room for clutter and no need for extras.

Jesus began his journey to Jerusalem during his forty days of testing in the desert at the beginning of his ministry. There's no mention in Scripture of any home comforts – no tent, no supplies of water, nothing to read. We are told simply that he was 'led' (*Matt 4:1*) or 'sent out' (*Mark 1:12*) by the Spirit. In that barren place, with only wild animals and angels for company, he was tested as to the means he would use in his Messiahship. Would he use his power for his own ends? Would he create a spectacle so that people followed him out of awe? Would he compromise with Satan? Jesus did not debate, but merely countered the temptations by quoting the word of God that was stored in his heart.

From that moment he was a man uncluttered, unencumbered by anything that would hold him back. He called those who followed him to travel light (*Luke 9:3–6*). He offered no travel insurance, issued no parachutes. They were to be dependent on the God who sent them out and on the hospitality of those to whom they were sent. In a life that is today characterised by 'things', such unclutteredness sounds appealing but a little naïve.

In this Lenten journey of the heart, are there things that we need to let go of, like autumn leaves that quietly fall at this time in the southern hemisphere? Red leaves of anger and shame? Green leaves of envy and jealousy? Yellow leaves of bitterness and resentment? Brown leaves of regret over spoiled dreams? Let them fall. Do a spring-clean of the heart.

Come, let us prepare for this Lenten journey by unpacking.

WEDNESDAY 13 MARCH
Coming Home to the Past

Genesis 33:1–11

'If I have found favour in your eyes, accept this gift from me.
For to see your face is like seeing the face of God, now that you
have received me favourably' (v. 10, NIV).

The story of Jacob and Esau is a story of deceit and discovery, and a story of home-coming. The Bible tells it frankly, that 'Isaac ... loved Esau, but Rebekah loved Jacob' (25:28). Jacob, the younger, cheated Esau out of his birthright and his father's blessing. Afraid that, on the death of Isaac, Esau would kill his brother in revenge, Rebekah tells Jacob to run for his life. He flees and goes to live with his uncle, Laban, where he stays for years, marrying Leah and Rachel and fathering children. Using his natural shrewdness and some unusual animal husbandry methods, Jacob becomes very prosperous, but finds that his father-in-law's attitude towards him gradually changes (31:2). Ill at ease, Jacob examines his options. He can stick it out where he is, he can strike out on his own with his wives, children and livestock, or he can return home and face the brother he had wronged years earlier. Genesis 31:3 says that the Lord tells Jacob to return home.

The Jacob who sets out to face his brother is not the same man who fled earlier. Jacob the deceiver has changed. This time he is honest with himself and fearful, and he begs God for help (see 32:9–12). That makes all the difference. No longer hiding and trying to trick his brother, Jacob faces his past as he heads for home. As he approaches Esau, he sends envoys and gifts to appease him. But instead of recrimination and revenge, Jacob finds welcome and forgiveness. As Esau embraces him, Jacob tells him it is like looking into the face of God (33:10). He discovers that the brother he has feared for all the years has changed, and with that discovery, Jacob is himself set free from his past.

Facing the past and owning up to who we are is part of our Lenten journey. It may not be easy or comfortable to face what we have left behind. But as we do, like Jacob, we may find ourselves looking into the face of God who embraces us and welcomes us home.

THURSDAY 14 MARCH
A Long Way from Home

Jeremiah 29:4–14

' "I know the plans I have for you," declares the LORD, "plans to prosper you and not to harm you, plans to give you hope and a future" ' (v. 11, NIV).

I have only ever once felt 'in exile' and that was in my own homeland. Forced to return home from missionary service because of ill health, I felt that God had brought me into exile from the place of his calling, rather than bringing me home. But verses from Jeremiah 29 about the plans of God even in the place of exile gave me hope.

The prophet Jeremiah was called by God to be a prophet to Judah, the southern kingdom. He confronted the leaders and the people with their sin and prophesied both their seventy-year captivity in Babylon and the fall of Jerusalem. His task was not popular, his words often ignored. But when he sent a letter from Jerusalem to the people in exile, he did not say, 'I told you so' or 'You're getting what you deserve.' Rather, he told them to see their exile as part of God's plan and urged them to use it as an opportunity to grow closer to God. They should settle down, he told them, build houses, plant gardens and even pray for their captors. In other words, they needed to accept that the land of exile was their new home from which they might never return.

This was not the sort of message the exiles wanted to hear. 'How can we sing the songs of the LORD while in a foreign land?' they asked, expressing the depth of despair and grief they were suffering (Ps 137:4). In that foreign land, far away from Jerusalem, the city of God, they felt as if God himself had abandoned them. They were not to know that, with the passage of time, their seemingly hopeless situation would give way to a new era of redemption and home-coming.

In a world that today seems full of people in exile – refugees, the unemployed, the war-torn, the homeless, the poverty-stricken – it is hard not to feel overwhelmed and hopeless. In whatever way we reach out to someone 'in exile' today, may Jeremiah's words help us to see God at work, restoring hope and bringing his people home.

FRIDAY 15 MARCH
Turning the Heart Towards Home

Luke 15:11–32

'He got up and went to his father. But while he was still a long way off, his father saw him and was filled with compassion for him; he ran to his son, threw his arms around him and kissed him' (v. 20, NIV).

The story of the prodigal son is the greatest home-coming story ever told. Simply put, it is the story of waste and grace.

A man had two sons. The younger asked for his inheritance before it was appropriate to have it. After all, his father was still alive. Asking for the money was like saying, 'I wish you were dead, Dad.' But the father gave it anyway. The lad left with his head full of plans and his pockets full of money. In a far country he squandered the lot. A famine in the land and hunger in his stomach drove him to feeding pigs, an unthinkable task for a Jewish person. As he watched the pigs eating and felt his own hunger, a memory of the abundance of home stirred within him.

With a speech playing over and over in his mind, he began the long walk home. His plan was to work for his father, earn enough money to pay back what he had wasted and then maybe talk reconciliation. But at the edge of the village he was met by his father who had long been watching and waiting for his home-coming. Throwing aside all dignity, the father had gathered up his robes and run to meet the son before the condemning comments of the other villagers could turn him away. The young man was only able to get out part of his speech before the father ordered a robe, a ring and sandals – all the symbols of welcome – to be brought to him. A feast was prepared to celebrate the home-coming of a son who had been given up for dead.

Whether we feel prodigal or not, this story of waste and grace is our story as well. Whether I have chosen to leave home and waste my inheritance or, like the older brother, stay home and be dutiful, I too stand in need of grace. This story is the good news of a God who is a loving, pursuing, welcoming, grace-filled Father whose arms are always open and waiting for his children to come home.

SATURDAY 16 MARCH
Lazarus' Home-Coming

John 11:38–44

'When he had said this, Jesus called in a loud voice,
"Lazarus, come out!" ' (v. 43, NIV).

On his roundabout way to Jerusalem, Jesus hears that his friend Lazarus is sick. Against the better judgment of his disciples, he suggests that they return to Judea to visit Lazarus and his anxious sisters. Thomas speaks more truth than he realises when he says to the others, 'Let us also go, that we may die with him' (v. 16). This is a story of intriguing contrasts – light and darkness, life and death, belief and unbelief. Lazarus' death is to be a sign, a rehearsal as it were, of what will soon happen to Jesus himself. But only those with eyes to see will understand what it means.

Jesus loves Lazarus and his family, but he delays, much to the frustration of the waiting sisters. By the time Jesus and his followers arrive in Bethany, Lazarus is well dead and firmly entombed. It was considered that a body prematurely buried could survive for three days, but four days would be impossible. Mary stays in the house in the pose of mourning while Martha hastens to express her grief to Jesus. He speaks words of resurrection to her and then proceeds to demonstrate the resurrection of Lazarus.

Standing beside the dead man's tomb, he lifts his voice to God so that everyone can hear (v. 41). His words of prayer are thanksgiving rather than petition. It is as if these words come at the end of a long conversation about Lazarus that Jesus has been having with the Father, perhaps for the past four days. His prayer gives a glimpse of the constant open communication that was happening between them. He then calls to the dead man, 'Lazarus, come out!' Three words call him back to life and out of the tomb. As Lazarus shuffles out of the darkness and into the dazzling light of day, Jesus gives the order for his grave-clothes to be removed. 'Strip off death, Lazarus, stir up life! This is your home-coming day!'

To reflect on
Is there an area of your life that God calls out of death and back into life today?

SUNDAY 17 MARCH
When God Does Not Answer

Psalm 38

'Because of your wrath there is no health in my body; my bones
have no soundness because of my sin' (v. 3, NIV).

Psalm 38 is the prayer of a sick person. Unlike other psalms, such as Psalm 6, this one has no hint of healing or thanksgiving in anticipation of healing. It begins and ends with prayer, with no mention of God's intervention. It is as if the psalmist is reminding God of his continued affliction: 'No change. Situation still critical. Patient getting impatient!'

The psalmist seems to have almost every disease in the book – stinking open wounds, searing pain and weakness, internal organs in distress. He is as good as dead, crushed almost beyond healing. He blames God for his illness. His sin has incurred divine displeasure and the resultant illness has brought alienation both from God and from his former acquaintances.

Some years ago I met a woman who told me about her 'religious' upbringing, but how she had turned her back on the Church. Two years later, quite unexpectedly, she rang to tell me that 'the Almighty has dropped his clogs on me!' She was recovering from major surgery and facing ongoing treatment. Over the next few months we talked together as her illness worsened. Faith was a struggle, God still 'the Enemy'. But one day she told me that she had come to a point of having to decide whether there was a God and heaven or not. With a radiant face, she said she had decided that God was real and that heaven was going to be her next home. Having decided that with her mind, she threw her frail physical state into that belief. A few weeks later she died, with a serenity of spirit that comes when someone dies 'in the Lord'.

My friend's new-found faith and this psalmist's prayer speak a reality familiar to many sufferers today. God does not always answer prayer for healing the way we want him to, even when we pray desperate, fervent, faith-filled prayers. Why he does not is a mystery. But in the absence of an answer, the psalmist continues to rest his case with God. Prayer is the lifeline that he will not let go.

MONDAY 18 MARCH
Home Is Where the Heart Is

John 14:1–7

'Jesus answered, "I am the way and the truth and the life.
No-one comes to the Father except through me" ' (v. 6, NIV).

I grew up on lush farmland in the south of New Zealand. That was the place where the foundations of my life were laid. I go back there now and again and call it 'home'. My grandchildren live in another city and when I visit them I feel 'at home'. For three years my husband and I served in Zambia in the heart of Africa. We returned for a visit a few years ago and it was like 'going home'. Where is home for me? It is all these places and more, where people's lives have intersected with mine. My story is testimony to Jesus' promise that 'no one who has left home . . . for me and the gospel will fail to receive a hundred times as much' (Mark 10:29,30). Home is far more than place, it is people. Home is where the heart is.

For Jesus, home was even more than people. It was a Person. The Father was the one he had come from and the one he was going to. 'I came from you' (John 17:8) . . . 'I am coming to you' (17:11,13). Doing the will of his Father was his meat and drink, life and sustenance. His life of prayer was continual conversation with the Father. His miracles revealed the power of the Father.

His teaching showed the character of the Father. 'Anyone who has seen me,' he told Philip, 'has seen the Father' (14:9).

His mission to earth was to make the Father known (17:26). That mission, he told his disciples, would be completed in Jerusalem where he would be arrested, tried and crucified. That would be the final fulfilment of the Father's love. From there, he would be going home to the Father. In spite of all that lay ahead, Jesus never lost his sense of home. To his anxious disciples and to followers today who long for home, he says, 'Do not let your hearts be troubled . . . I am the way and the truth and the life . . . Follow me and I will lead you all the way home.'

TUESDAY 19 MARCH
Coming Home to Forgiveness

Colossians 3:12–17

'Forgive whatever grievances you may have against one another.
Forgive as the Lord forgave you' (v. 13, NIV).

One sunny day in the season of the pleasing but puzzling parables of the kingdom, Peter asked Jesus about forgiveness and how far it reached. 'Seven times over?' Peter suggested (*Matt 18:21*). One bitterly cold night, sitting in a bleak court-yard, Peter discovered that he needed forgiveness to reach much further than that (*Matt 26:75*). In response to Peter's question, Jesus told a story of forgiveness set in the context of grace. It was a story about a king, a servant and a debt. The point that Jesus made is that our debt to God is totally and forever beyond the possibility of payment. God's forgiveness reveals God's immeasurable grace.

Forgiveness has been described as 'the thorniest of issues'. In a world of instant commodities, forgiveness is a long journey, a slow return, and a home-coming as difficult for believers today as it was for the prodigal son. Jesus gave himself as an object lesson in forgiveness. Humiliated and in deep pain, as he hung on the cross he called on the Father's resources of forgiveness. 'Father, forgive them, for they do not know what they are doing' (*Luke 23:34*).

God's forgiveness extended to us insists that we look at others through the eyes of mercy. Forgiveness is restoration and reconciliation. Forgiveness is right relationship, restored at cost. It lies behind the desire of a young South African to meet with the people who had killed her father, 'so that I can forgive them'. It lies behind the ability of a pastor to conduct the wedding of a young man who had killed the pastor's son. Such forgiveness can only be described as an act of grace. It reaches beyond the narrow boundaries of our hearts, beyond the meagre measure of our compassion, even beyond the depth of our own pain. But we cannot offer it to others until we have found our way home to the table that has been lavishly spread for us with God's forgiveness. God calls us home to his forgiveness today.

To reflect on
Forgiveness is the fragrance that flowers breathe when they are trampled on.

WEDNESDAY 20 MARCH

An Open Home

John 12:1–2

'Six days before the Passover, Jesus arrived at Bethany, where Lazarus lived, whom Jesus had raised from the dead' (v. 1, NIV).

Jesus warned an inquirer one day that, in contrast to foxes who had holes to sleep in, the Son of God had nowhere to lay his head (*Matt 8:20*). For this would-be follower at least, discipleship came with no guarantee of the most basic necessity – shelter. The Scriptures tell of no home that Jesus owned or used as his permanent base of operations. Did he doss down in a dinghy night after night? Or was he dependent on contacts through the disciples of a home here and there, dotted along the landscape of his journey?

Mention is made of only one home where we catch a sense of warm familiarity – the home of Mary, Martha and Lazarus at Bethany. On the final leg of his journey to Jerusalem he comes to their home once again. There is Lazarus, recently dead and now very much alive. There is Martha, doing what she does best, preparing a meal. And there is Mary, gazing in wondering love at Jesus and waiting for her moment to offer her final fragrant act of love.

With all that lay up ahead, did Jesus take one long last look at this house that had been a refuge for him? Did he wander out into the quiet garden? Did he remember the times when he had come physically exhausted, spiritually depleted, 'peopled out'? Did he recall times of gentle laughter, nourishing food and uninterrupted sleep that had recharged his batteries and enabled him to move out once more into the world of shrieking demons and slow-witted disciples?

The comfort-loving part of me longs for that to be so for Jesus. Oh the joy of a room, such as Elijah had, where he was welcomed and cared for (*1 Kgs 17*). Oh the comfort of homes that have been opened to God's servants simply because they are God's servants. This Lent as we travel with Jesus to Jerusalem, let us identify with gratitude those places where we most feel 'at home' and let us offer an open door of hospitality to another pilgrim on the way who may be weary.

THURSDAY 21 MARCH
A Zacchaeus Heart

Luke 19:1–9

'Jesus said to him, "Today salvation has come to this house, because this man, too, is a son of Abraham" ' (v. 9, NIV).

Zacchaeus is a man who came home to himself on a memorable day when Jesus visited him. Every Sunday school child knows two things about Zacchaeus – he was short and he was shady! But Jesus saw beyond the physical to the heart of the man. On another day Jesus looked into the heart of another rich young man, offered him a choice, then watched in sadness as he turned and walked away (18:18–24). Somewhere between these two stories, my story is told.

I long to have a Zacchaeus heart this Lent. Even though I hide from God (under the pretext of getting a better view of what he's doing), I'm glad to be noticed. I want to hear him call my name, just as he called to Zacchaeus. I'm delighted to be singled out for special attention. God inviting himself to my house is a peculiar honour for me. He didn't wait to be invited, but paid me the honour of inviting himself! I'm excited, nervous, a bit of a dither really. I hope everyone notices as we walk home together.

But it's one thing to be like Zacchaeus when all the world is watching. It's another thing when God and I come inside and shut the door on the world. It's not always so comfortable then. My Zacchaeus house doesn't stand up easily to close scrutiny of the God kind. He notices things I wish I had had time to hide: my choice in reading material, the clutter of my heart. He talks about disturbing things, like priorities and passions. He offers me choices and changes. He sits quietly with my silence and shame. He gazes deeply but so lovingly that his truth cannot be resisted. I look around and, for once, see things as they really are. His look enables me to look at myself. His call gives me strength to make amends and start over again. His love and forgiveness somehow make my house into a home.

Jesus, on your way to Jerusalem, please will you come and stay at my house today?

85

FRIDAY 22 MARCH

Longing for Home

Hebrews 11:8–16

'All these people were still living by faith when they died. They did not receive the things promised; they only saw them and welcomed them from a distance' (v. 13, NIV).

I knew a retired Salvation Army officer some years ago who seemed to be the epitome of holiness. He was a saint of a man, radiant with the presence of God. But the closer he got to heaven, the further away he felt. He told me one day it was like feeling homesick all the time, living on earth but longing for heaven.

The Scriptures give a long list of people who lived on earth but with heaven in their hearts. They were people who lived by faith, hearing a different call from the insistent voices of the world around them, listening to different music of the heart, following a different way of life. They put up with all kinds of suffering because they knew that it was only temporary. They lived with impermanence and change, symbolised by their tent dwellings, because they had a vision of a city with strong and permanent foundations. Their hearts were not anchored to the things of this world, but were joined by a strong rope of faith to the next. 'They admitted,' the writer to the Hebrews says, 'that they were aliens and strangers on earth ... longing for a better country – a heavenly one' (vv. 13,16).

Jesus lived with a pilgrim heart all through his earthly life and especially as he moved towards Jerusalem. A yearning to be with his Father drew him on, even though he knew that his home-coming would be through suffering and death. Like my retired friend, Jesus longed for heaven while living on earth.

An ancient Aztec Indian prayer acknowledges that life is short and everything is merely 'on loan'.

We take life in your painting us, and we breathe in your singing us.
But only for so short a while have you loaned us to each other.

Our call today is to live with a pilgrim heart, receiving all of life as a gift, merely on loan and holding it with open hands. In an ever-changing world, the unchanging love of God, as shown to us in Jesus, beckons our homesick hearts and draws us home.

SATURDAY 23 MARCH
An Act of Anointing

John 12:1–8

'Then Mary took about a pint of pure nard, an expensive perfume;
she poured it on Jesus' feet and wiped his feet with her hair. And the
house was filled with the fragrance of the perfume' (v. 3, NIV).

For a long time her eyes were on Jesus. She was used to sitting at his feet and looking up into his face. She had seen that face on days when he was relaxed and laughter had filled the room. She had recently seen his face wet with tears as they had stood together at Lazarus' grave. Now here he was at a dinner party given in his honour, but there was no light-hearted banter, no life-of-the-party stories from him today. Even as he re-clined at the table with his friends, she could see shadows in his eyes. For the hundredth time, she ran her hand over the cold, smooth surface of her perfume flask.

Then, at a sudden lull in the conversation, she moved forward silently. As she knelt at his feet, her loosened hair cascaded down, hiding her face and her tears as she poured the perfume over his feet. Such strong, bony feet! She was familiar with his face, but she had never touched his feet before. With intimate hands she massaged the fragrant nard oil into his skin and between his toes, around his heels and ankles. There was too much oil and she wiped it with her hair, trying to absorb it. Her hair became a towel as she wiped again and again. With one last massage of his feet, she held them both for a moment in a silent act of blessing and then, for the first time, looked up into his eyes that had been watching her.

It was only as she looked up that she became aware of a murmur around the table that mingled with the heavy fragrance of oil. There was a clucking of disapproving tongues and the sound of words like 'waste' and 'cost'. She heard her sister Martha sob, 'Mary, how could you?' And it sounded like Judas spouting forth about 'money that should have been given to the poor'. But as she looked into Jesus' face, she saw that the shadows were gone from his eyes. They were now shining with a silent 'thank you'.

SUNDAY 24 MARCH

Ride on, Ride on in Majesty!

John 12:12–19

'They took palm branches and went out to meet him, shouting, "Hosanna! Blessed is he who comes in the name of the Lord!" ' (v. 13, NIV).

On the first day of the week, this day known as Palm Sunday, Jesus rides into Jerusalem on a donkey. The city is teeming with pilgrims who have come for the Passover festival, the commemoration of God's deliverance of his people from Egypt. Hearing that Jesus is 'on the way', they go out to welcome him, lining the streets with palm branches and filling the air with a chorus of 'Hosannas' (Save us!) and with songs of blessing. With unrestrained joy they turn on a welcome that is fit for a king. The crowd greets a monarch for whom they have long waited and who they believe will purge the nation of foreign domination and revive the ancient glories of Israel. *'Ride on, ride on in majesty!'*

He is indeed a king. He comes to bring peace to the nations. He comes to overturn oppression and domination. But it is on a donkey that he comes, not a snorting white charger. Trailing behind him in his triumphal entry is not a train of captives but a struggling, straggling band of disciples who are still slow to understand what is happening. He comes, not to set up a rival kingdom to Caesar's, but to suffer and die. Within a week he will be led out of the city as a defeated captive. He comes as a king who will be crowned with thorns, enthroned on a cross and hailed as the chief of fools. *'Ride on, ride on in majesty, In lowly pomp ride on to die.'*

In the midst of the deafening applause we witness the terrible loneliness of a pale figure on a quiet donkey, weeping for his people. On this Palm Sunday we too raise our voices in welcome and worship. We hail him as one who comes to die for our sins, one who comes to be bound in order that we might be set free.

Ride on, ride on in majesty!
In lowly pomp ride on to die;
Bow thy meek head to mortal pain,
Then take, O God, thy power, and reign.
Henry Hart Milman SASB 150

MONDAY 25 MARCH

Passion Week

Romans 8:28–39

'If God is for us, who can be against us? He who did not spare his own Son, but gave him up for us all – how will he not also, along with him, graciously give us all things?' (vv. 31,32, NIV).

The week leading up to Jesus' crucifixion is called Holy Week or Passion Week. The word 'passion' comes from the Latin word *pascho*, meaning 'to be done to'. It is the opposite of the word *poio*, which means 'to do'. In life there is action (things that we do) and there is passion (things that are done to us).

From the beginning of the gospel accounts, Jesus has been portrayed as a man of action, moving with confident, deliberate stride from one life-changing encounter, one miraculous healing, one decisive word to the next. As he has journeyed towards Jerusalem the pace of his stride has slowed, but he is still a man on the move, focused and free, always majestically in charge. The triumphal entry into Jerusalem on Palm Sunday is the climax of his action. As he enters the city, the crowd sings their praises – 'Hosanna, blessed is he who comes in the name of the Lord!' But from this day on, a life of action changes dramatically into a life of passion. During this Holy Week, Jesus becomes the one handed over, done

to, acted upon. Judas hands Jesus over to the Jewish leaders. They in turn hand him over to Pilate who then hands him over to the will of the people. As the chant of 'Hosanna' changes to a cry of 'Crucify!', Jesus is handed over to arrest, whipping, interrogation, sentencing, spitting, stripping and finally death.

But this handing over is neither defeat nor reason for despair. This is the story of redemption. Over thirty years earlier, Abba God had handed over a baby to Mary and Joseph to care for. Jesus' whole life was a handing over. Even in death he freely handed himself over, giving himself up, choosing to be the suffering Messiah, the Saviour of the world. The handing over that began in a cradle now ends on a cross.

Pray today for someone you know who is being 'handed over' – a patient in hospital, an elderly person in residential care, someone awaiting trial.

TUESDAY 26 MARCH

Washed Feet, Broken Bread, Poured-Out Wine

John 13:1–17

'Now that you know these things, you will be blessed if you do them'
(v. 17, NIV).

There is one last thing for Jesus to do, one last handing over. In the Upper Room the meal is being served, the rich aroma of the food mingling with the dark intentions of Judas. Jesus gets up from the table, wraps a towel around his waist, pours water into a basin and begins to wash the disciples' feet. Wordlessly, he moves from one to the other – Andrew, Philip, James, Judas. Does he take an especially long time washing Judas' feet? There is a deep silence in the room, apart from the gentle splashing of water and the private words that he speaks to each one in turn.

Peter is flushed and agitated as Jesus kneels before him. He bursts out, 'Lord, this isn't right. It's not your place to wash my feet.'

Jesus pauses and then says, 'Peter, are you going to be too proud to let me do this for you? If you are, I have to tell you, you will lose everything.'

'Oh Master!' Peter cries. 'Wash me, but not just my feet. Wash my hands and my head as well!' And as Jesus stoops to wash his feet, Peter weeps.

When he finishes, Jesus puts the basin in the corner, takes off the towel, puts his robe back on and sits down. Gathering everyone together with his eyes, he says, 'What I have done for you today, you are now to do for others.'

The other gospel writers do not mention this foot-washing, but they do describe how Jesus takes bread, the symbol of God's faithfulness, blesses and breaks it and offers it to them. 'Take and eat, this is my body' (*Matt 26:26*). Then taking the cup of wine he gives thanks and passes it to them, saying, 'Drink from it, all of you. This is my blood . . . poured out for many for the forgiveness of sins' (*Matt 26:27,28*). They have seen these hands bless and break bread before, but this time as he hands it to them, it is as if, in a way beyond their understanding, they are receiving his very life.

WEDNESDAY 27 MARCH
Judas Hands Him Over

Mark 14:10–11, 43–46

'The chief priests . . . were delighted . . . and promised to give him money. So he watched for an opportunity to hand him over' (vv. 10,11, NIV).

Mark places the account of Judas going to the chief priests straight after the story of the woman anointing Jesus with perfume. A beautiful act of love is followed by a dark act of betrayal. Her intimate embrace of his feet is contrasted with Judas' cold kiss of identification in the garden of Gethsemane. Neither act will ever be forgotten.

I want to shake him and scream, 'How could you, Judas? Despicable little man that you are, how could you do what you did? How could you live so closely with someone all that time, carry his trust, feel his power, witness his miracles and still not understand? How could you listen but not hear? Watch but not see? How could you learn so much but, at the last, fail the test? How could you, Judas?'

Mark offers no explanation at all. Luke says that Satan entered him. Matthew claims that greed was his motive. Some scholars have argued that Judas was a devoted disciple whose loyalty towards Jesus cooled for various reasons. Perhaps he misunderstood from the very beginning, believing that Jesus was going to overturn the oppressive Roman rule. Perhaps he

was disillusioned by Jesus' apparent inactivity and believed that handing him over would finally force him to act.

Whatever his motive, one haunting question stands unanswered. Is there redemption for Judas? Is there any hope for a man who handed the Son of God over to death, since God purposed his death anyway? Catherine Baird, Salvation Army poet, says there is one word for Judas, one point in his favour.

He took all the blame for vileness . . .
And he did not point at me!

If Judas, one of the Twelve, could betray his Master for no other reason except greed or Satan, then I too have the potential to hand him over. Is there redemption for Judas? Please God, let there be so, for if there is redemption for him, then maybe there is redemption for me as well!

'Killing Jesus was like trying to destroy a dandelion seed-head by blowing on it.'

Walter Wink

THURSDAY 28 MARCH
Pilate Hands Him Over

Mark 15:1–15

'The chief priests . . . turned him over to Pilate. He had Jesus flogged, and handed him over to be crucified' (vv. 1,15, NIV).

Peter hands over his Lord with his embarrassed denials, Judas hands him over with his kiss, and the religious leaders hand him over, physically bound, to Pilate. As Roman governor, Pilate would have no interest in putting a native Jew on trial simply because he had violated Jewish religious regulations. A charge that Jesus had declared himself to be the Messiah would be of no concern to Pilate. But a charge that he has called himself the king of the Jews was a serious political matter. A claim to be king was a crime against the sovereign power of Rome.

Pilate suspects that the high priests have handed him over out of envy but he questions Jesus about the claim to kingship. Much to Pilate's consternation, Jesus chooses to answer with a verbal shrug and then remains silent. Pilate cannot release someone who refuses to answer such a serious charge and so hands him over to the will of the crowd. Stirred up by the chief priests, the crowd reminds Pilate of the custom of releasing a prisoner at the time of the feast. Seeing this as his easy way out,

Pilate assumes that they will call for the release of Jesus, but the spotlight falls on Barabbas.

Barabbas had been arrested for committing murder in an insurrection. He may have been a right-wing extremist fighting to deliver Israel from the pollution of Roman rule, or he may have simply been a bandit, a type of heroic Robin Hood figure, loved by the poor. The crowd chooses release for Barabbas but crucifixion for Jesus. When Pilate asks, 'Why?' they scream their demand even louder.

Barabbas, handed over to the crowd, goes free. Jesus, handed over to the crowd, goes to the cross. The crowd in their fickleness chooses the one who takes the lives of others and condemns the one who gives his life for others. Pilate leaves himself no choice but to hand over the Son of God.

To reflect on
The one who called God 'Abba' (Daddy) dies in place of Barabbas, son of 'Daddy' – an unknown father.

FRIDAY 29 MARCH
One Tree Hill

Mark 15:21–32

'They brought Jesus to the place called Golgotha
(which means The Place of the Skull)' (v. 22, NIV).

One day not so long ago, all eyes in Auckland, New Zealand's largest city, were on a lone tree standing on a high hill. The landmark Monterey pine had stood on One Tree Hill for 125 years. In old photos of the city that tree provided a familiar point of reference. Tourists flocked to view the city from its vantage point. The Irish band U2 immortalised the spot in their song 'One Tree Hill' in memory of one of their members, a New Zealander who died in a motorcycle accident in Dublin in 1986. That Monterey pine became an icon for a city that looked on it as its own.

However, two chainsaw attacks in recent years and damage from strong winds had made the tree unsafe, and the decision was made to remove it. The day it was felled was like a day of mourning for the city of Auckland. From before dawn, people gathered to watch. A local Maori iwi (tribe) performed a ceremony before workers with chainsaws moved in. The biggest cuts of wood were set aside for display or carving while spectators wanting a souvenir scavenged the smaller pieces. It was top item on the six o'clock news where the tree's 'spectacular felling' amidst a 'festival atmosphere' was described in expansive language.

On another day, a long time ago, a group of people watched another tree on another hill. The atmosphere was far from festival. Some of the spectators merely watched and wondered. Others were silent and numb with grief at a crucifixion they had been warned about, but could not comprehend. For hours the surrounding area was plunged into eerie darkness. It seemed that even God had turned his back on that tree and the battered human figure nailed to it.

Today the spot is empty. The tree is gone. The work has been completed. Jesus, the Son of God who suffered and died that day for the sins of the world, is now seated at the right hand of God where he prays for you (*Col 3:1*).

From Golgotha to Glory! Hallelujah!

SATURDAY 30 MARCH
Tomb Watching

John 19:38–42

'At the place where Jesus was crucified, there was a garden,
and in the garden a new tomb, in which no-one had ever been laid'
(v. 41, NIV).

Jesus has died. Joseph of Arimathea, a member of the Jewish council and secret follower of Jesus, goes boldly to Pilate and asks permission to take Jesus' body down from the cross. Somewhat unusually, Pilate releases the body to Joseph, even though he is not a relative. Nicodemus, likewise a member of the council and a quiet follower, helps Joseph to wrap the body with a kingly amount of spices in bandage-like strips of linen. With gentle, respectful hands they do their final anointing of the Anointed One and then lay him in a newly cut rock tomb. The other Gospels mention that some of the women followers, including the two Marys and Salome, are close by, watching.

An artist has painted a picture of the body of Jesus wrapped in a traditional white shroud, lying on a stone slab. All around are sorrowing angels keeping watch. Their soft rainbow colours contrast with the darkness of the tomb. Their heads are bowed, their hearts weary with sadness. They hold silent vigil, waiting for the blinding light of resurrection to banish the gloom of death.

The vigil of the women at the tomb and the angels in the artist's picture express the tone of this day. This in-between day is a day for quiet breathing, restful watching and waiting. Some churches hold a 'tomb watch' on Easter Saturday, when people enter a darkened room and hold vigil there. Maybe we all need a 'tomb watch' every now and then. Maybe we need to keep vigil for a part of ourselves that feels dead or lost or has fallen into a dark tomb of depression or despair. Our loss may be an intimate friendship, a physical strength, the ability to forgive someone. Our 'tomb watch' may be for someone else in their pain. As we wait in the darkness, let us prepare to welcome the light.

To reflect on
In the midst of the grey sorrow of this day, there is yet a tinge of colour and hope: 'At the place where Jesus was crucified, there was a garden . . .' (v. 41).

SUNDAY 31 MARCH
Resurrection Morning

John 20:1–9

'Early on the first day of the week, while it was still dark, Mary Magdalene went to the tomb and saw that the stone had been removed from the entrance. So she came running . . .' (v. 1, NIV).

Christ the Lord is risen today – Hallelujah! After grey days of denial, bitter insults and dashed hopes, we are catapulted on this resurrection morning to a brightness beyond our imagining. The cold dark places of the tomb are thrown wide open and shown to be empty. The tears of sorrow wept by those who loved him best are now changed to tears of joy. The Lord is risen! He is risen indeed!

This is a day to be experienced 'in contrast'. We cannot catch the deep joy of this Easter Sunday unless we have carried the deep sadness of Good Friday. We cannot appreciate the light until we have sat for a time in darkness. Delight is deepest when despair has been most profound.

The Easter contrast happened in my life. My childhood Easters were coloured cold comfortless grey. Every year it was the same, no matter what the weather. There was something about Easter that was dark, oppressive and far too grown-up for me to comprehend. In my childish way, I figured that if only I could hold my breath from Good Friday until the sun exploded out again on Easter Sunday, I'd be okay.

It took the birth of my first child and the death of my mother, two weeks apart, right on top of Easter, to put colour into Easter for me. In one broad stroke of family joy and grief, the message of Easter came alive as I saw that birth and death, light and darkness, joy and sorrow, are parts of each other and inseparable parts of the Easter story.

What colour is forgiveness? What colour are bursting hearts that were so recently discouraged? What colour is joy? This is drama painted in colours that refuse to be muted – the colours of a God who identifies with our brokenness, forgives our fallenness, transforms our sorrows into joy and gives us a new beginning every day. Come, celebrate the vibrant colours of Easter Sunday. This is a story of hope, explosive hope, to take your very breath away!

MONDAY 1 APRIL
The Easter Mystery

Colossians 1:24–29

'To them God has chosen to make known among the Gentiles the glorious riches of this mystery, which is Christ in you, the hope of glory' (v. 27, NIV).

Holy Week was filled with sounds, tastes, smells and sights – the roaring crowd on Jerusalem's streets; the clatter of silver pieces; the heavy fragrance of perfume; the taste of bitter wine; the sounds of arrest, trial, flogging and crucifixion; the roll of the dice, and of the heavy stone across the entrance to the tomb. For all its drama, the last week of Jesus' life speaks of a world with which we are familiar. In our mind's eye we can picture the scene, hear the noises, smell the fragrance of perfume and passion. But with the coming week – resurrection week – it's as if a new lens is put on the camera. The events after Jesus' resurrection have an otherworld, sepia-like quality to them.

There is the upper room where he suddenly appears, ghostlike, to his disciples who are hiding in fear. Unghostlike, he says he is hungry and asks for some fish to eat. There are the grieving friends on their way to Emmaus who don't recognise him. Others come in from a night's fishing, and find him on the beach with breakfast ready.

These appearances are full of mystery. They are hard to understand. But the mystery is part of our faith. It beckons us on to a future, to a God whom as yet we can only glimpse. Paul, writing later, said, 'We don't yet see things clearly. We're squinting in a fog, peering through a mist. But it won't be long before the weather clears and the sun shines bright! We'll see it all then, see it all as clearly as God sees us' (1 Cor 13:12, The Message).

So what to do with the mystery? I believe we need to hold tightly in one hand the certainties of our faith – the things we can be sure of. And with the other hand open, we need to hold the mysteries, let them lead us on as we seek answers and understanding.

Today, let us thank God for the certainties of what we know, and trust him for the mysteries that will one day be made clear.

TUESDAY 2 APRIL
A Light in the Darkness

John 20:10–18

'Mary stood outside the tomb crying. As she wept, she bent over to look into the tomb' (v. 11, NIV).

In the fresh light of early dawn, Mary Magdalene comes to the tomb and finds that the heavy stone has been rolled back from the entrance. John's account says that she turns and runs straight back to tell Peter and John that the body of Jesus has gone. They come running, see the signs of resurrection, then hurry home as quickly as they came, leaving Mary alone.

Like another Mary weeping at a loved one's tomb (see 11:32–35), this Mary's heart is broken. She was a woman who loved greatly because she had been greatly forgiven. Her life had been transformed when Jesus cast seven demons out of her (see Mark 16:9). She stood at the cross when Jesus died, while all the other disciples except John were hiding in fear. She comes to his tomb on this early morning to anoint his body with burial spices, and thus offer her last act of love.

In spite of her tears, she bends over to look into the darkness of the tomb. There she sees two angels sitting where his body had been. Turning, she speaks to Jesus himself, not recognising him but assuming him to be the gardener who has removed the body. As Jesus speaks her name, 'Mary', she cries out in joyful recognition. He tells her not to hold on to him but to go and tell what she has seen.

In grieving, stooping, recognising and telling, Mary faced her own resurrection. She did not run away from her grief, but faced it head-on, looking into the very depths of its darkness. She stepped into the dark tomb because Jesus had already stepped with forgiveness into the dark sin of her life. She had already faced the tragedy of the crucifixion and so could now experience the joy of the resurrection. She did not need to hold Jesus to herself, but was able to let him be free and thus let the glorious news out to the world.

A prayer for today
Risen One, come meet with me in the garden of my life.

WEDNESDAY 3 APRIL
When Hopes Lie Shattered

Luke 24:13–35

'When he was at the table with them, he took bread, gave thanks, broke it and began to give it to them. Then their eyes were opened . . .' (vv. 30,31a, NIV).

The encounter between Jesus and the two disciples on the road to Emmaus is one of the most vivid resurrection appearances. The disciples have been in Jerusalem for the Passover and now head home, their hearts heavy, their feet like lead. They have witnessed the death by crucifixion of their beloved Jesus and, with his death, their hopes for Israel's redemption. Their heads are down, their discussion animated as they walk, so they neither notice nor recognise the stranger who suddenly joins them. When he asks them about their sorrow, they are amazed that any–one could be unaware of the recent happenings in Jerusalem. They proceed to tell the stranger about 'Jesus of Nazareth, a prophet powerful in word and deed before God and all the people'. They tell of his crucifixion, with their an–guished cry, 'But we had hoped . . .'

This cry of shattered hope is repeated every time a young marriage breaks, a child becomes terminally ill, a son or daughter of the family fails to live out their glowing potential. 'But we had hoped!' When the heart cries and an aching void of grief engulfs, we too share the journey with these two on their way to Emmaus.

The stranger listens, questions and explains; then, when they come to their destination, he accepts their invitation to come and eat with them. As he takes the bread, gives thanks, breaks it and hands it to them, they recall another day when bread was broken and offered in the same way. In the moment of recognising Jesus, he is gone. Suddenly their hearts are no longer heavy, their hopes are fresh and alive, and with feet as light as wings they hurry back to Jerusalem. For these two, the news of Jesus' resurrection changes heaviness to hope, despair to delight, fear to faith. May it be so for strugglers and sufferers today.

To reflect on
The resurrection proves that:

- *truth is stronger than falsehood*
- *good is stronger than evil*
- *love is stronger than hatred*
- *life is stronger than death.'*

William Barclay

THURSDAY 4 APRIL
Too Good to be True

John 20:24–29

'The other disciples told him, "We have seen the Lord!" But he said to them, "Unless I see the nail marks in his hands and put my finger where the nails were, and put my hand into his side, I will not believe it" ' (v. 25, NIV).

Thomas had missed the last gathering of the disciples. Grief and failure had knocked all the wind out of him, and after the crucifixion he had turned his face to the wall and tried to sleep the nightmare away. Even when Andrew banged on his door and yelled out that Jesus was alive, he had retorted, 'I'll believe that when I see it!' But there comes a point when a man can sleep no longer, and hunger in his stomach and curiosity in his heart get him going again.

It wasn't that he didn't want to believe. It was, well, that he felt responsible for what had happened. After all, when Jesus had talked about going to Jerusalem for Passover this year and they had not been able to dissuade him, it was he, Thomas, who had said with bravado, 'Then let's all go and die with him.' But when Jesus died, Thomas had fled in the darkness like all the others, scared stiff!

He climbed the stairs to the upper room and as he got to the door it suddenly swung open and Peter lurched out. His face lit up when he saw Thomas. He grabbed him by the arm and pulled him into the room. A chorus of welcoming voices broke out all around him. Matthew was there, and Andrew. They were all there, in fact, except Judas, of course. Thomas started to explain where he had been, when he suddenly realised that they were looking at something behind him. Curious, he turned, and as he turned, he heard a familiar voice saying, 'Peace be with you.' It was Jesus.

Thomas stared in disbelief. Jesus spoke directly to him, 'Thomas, put your finger on the wounds on my hands and in my side. What you've been told is true. I'm alive.' Jesus stood there, holding out his hands. With tears of joy streaming down his face, Thomas fell on his knees and cried, 'My Lord and my God!'

To reflect on
For Thomas, seeing was believing. For Christians today, faith means believing even when we cannot see.

FRIDAY 5 APRIL

Breakfast on the Shore

John 21:1–14

'Jesus said to them, "Come and have breakfast." None of the disciples dared ask him, "Who are you?" They knew it was the Lord' (v. 12, NIV).

John's account of the seven disciples going fishing is told factually, with no hint of the feelings and emotions of the group. Peter was not necessarily giving in to despair and returning to his old way of life. His decision may be simply a practical response to the fact that people still need to eat. Besides, there may be something reassuring for Peter and the others in doing a familiar task that allows them space for thinking through the recent cataclysmic events.

As happened on another occasion (see *Luke 5:5*), they catch nothing and are heading for shore when they see a waiting figure. The figure directs them to go back out again and to throw their nets on to the right side of the boat. Does a memory stir of that same voice giving that same instruction after an earlier unsuccessful fishing trip? They obey the instruction and, almost immediately it seems, catch a net-full. The ever-intuitive John recognises Jesus. Characteristically, he tells Peter, and, equally characteristically, Peter throws himself into the sea, not to bring the fish to shore but to reach the Lord as quickly as he can. This scene sounds like John and Peter at the empty tomb all over again (*20:4–8*). Peter wraps his outer garment around himself, a curious thing to do before jumping into the water. But he may have been preparing himself to greet the Lord and a greeting was considered to be a religious act that one could do only when clothed.

On the shore, a fire is burning with fish cooking. Bread is prepared. Where it had all come from, and why the disciples still seem reticent about Jesus, are all part of the Easter mystery. 'Is it really you?' they long to ask. It is he and yet it is not he as they have known him before. Jesus breaks bread and hands it and the fish to them to eat. Again we are not told how they felt, but can sense that this food, as on another occasion (*6:12*) would satisfy far more than their physical hunger.

SATURDAY 6 APRIL
A Question of Love

John 21:15–19

'Peter was hurt because Jesus asked him the third time, "Do you love me?" He said, "Lord, you know all things; you know that I love you." Jesus said, "Feed my sheep" ' (v. 17, NIV).

Breakfast is over. Jesus speaks privately with Peter. 'Do you love me?' he asks, not once but three times. The repeated questioning gives the impression that Jesus is not convinced by Peter's response. But it could be that the three questions and their answers put to rest another bitter threesome from another bitter day. 'You're not one of his disciples, are you?' asked a servant girl and then a fellow by the fire. 'I am not,' he had said emphatically. 'Didn't I see you with him in the olive grove?' a servant had challenged. Again Peter had denied it.

Before the crucifixion, the relationship between these two men was one of love and trust. Jesus had chosen and prepared Peter for responsible leadership. But with Jesus' trial and death, that relationship was ruptured, leaving Peter shattered, grief-stricken, haunted by guilt. He must have known that his repeated disavowals had disqualified him from being a disciple of Jesus, let alone a leader. For Jesus, the heart of the matter is the question of love. 'Peter, do you love me?' he asks three times. The former

brash Peter is gone. Now humbled and embarrassed, he can only appeal to the Lord's knowledge that he truly loves him, in spite of failure. More than that, he cannot say. But more than that he need not say. His love for his Lord is to be shown in his care for the Lord's flock. His following will be costly.

Archbishop Oscar Romero of San Salvador spoke while celebrating mass: 'As a pastor I am obliged by divine command to give my life for those whom I love, and that is for all Salvadorans, even for those who may assassinate me. If the threats should come to pass, I offer God, from this very moment, my blood for the redemption and resurrection of El Salvador.' Not long afterwards, he was assassinated.

Your calling, and mine, will be worked out differently from how it was for Peter or Archbishop Romero, but the calling is exactly the same:

- *'Feed my lambs.'*
- *'Take care of my sheep.'*
- *'Follow me!'*

SUNDAY 7 APRIL

My Hope Is in You, Lord

Psalm 39

'Hear my prayer, O LORD, listen to my cry for help; be not deaf to my weeping. For I dwell with you as an alien, a stranger, as all my fathers were' (v. 12, NIV).

Yesterday's paper reported the death by shooting of three Palestinian teenagers in the troubled Middle East. Yesterday was the 102nd birthday of a frail resident at a nearby eventide home. For some, life is too short; for some, it is too long.

Psalm 39 is a powerful portrayal of life as it really is – full of contradictions. The psalmist begins, 'I said', and then states his intention not to speak. Like Job, he wants to avoid the sin of accusing God of wrongdoing (Job 1:22). Further, he does not want to give the wicked any ammunition for their attacks against him. So he keeps silence, but his words burn within him like heartburn and finally burst forth. Unlike Job, he does not curse the day of his birth, but focuses on his own life, concluding that it is 'as nothing before you'. Life, he says, is a mere handbreadth. This measurement was of four fingers (see Jer 52:21), one of the smallest in the Hebrew measuring system. As a metaphor it describes human life as something infinitesimal from God's perspective.

Having moved from silence to speech, he now moves from despair at the shortness of human life to an expression of hope. Verse 7, the exact centre of the psalm, represents a turning point. He confesses his sin and makes a humble request for forgiveness. Having begun in silence, he now asks God not to be silent to his weeping. But, at the same time, he asks him to look away.

The psalm seems to be full of contradictions – silence and speech, despair and hope, 'hear' and 'listen', then 'look away'. But this is surely reality. For many people, hope and despair do stand side by side. Life is both woeful and wonderful. But no matter how short – just to teenage years – or how long – even to 102 – we live as strangers, passing guests in this world (see Heb 11:13). Our call in the midst of all the uncertainties and ambiguities is to entrust our life and future to God.

Prayer
Today, Lord, my hope is in you.

THE BLESSED ONES
Introduction

I've been praying blessing prayers for as long as I can remember. 'Lord, bless my family, my friends, my work colleagues. Bless those who are in trouble today. Bless those who are serving you in difficult places. And Lord, please bless me as well.' The blessings I've had in mind as I've prayed have been for fullness, peace, contentment, refreshment – all the positive things I can possibly want for someone else, as well as for myself.

A closer look at Jesus' Sermon on the Mount and his words of blessing, however, has brought a startling revelation to me. I suddenly realise that I've been translating blessing in quite a different way from Jesus' use of the word. I've thought of blessing as fullness and abundance, but Jesus is reported here as saying that the truly blessed are the ones who are empty, poor, mourners and meek ones and those who are hungry and thirsty. Have I been praying for the wrong thing, then? Do I need to start asking God to make my friends and family – and myself – poor, hungry and empty?

This sermon on blessedness must surely be another example of the sacred paradoxes of Jesus:

- Do you want to have? Then give away what you have!
- Do you want to be first? Then take the last place!
- Do you want to be full? Then empty yourself out for others!

The best way I can explore these blessings is to see them revealed in people I know. So with this brief series on the beatitudes, I introduce you to some of my friends. Until recently I may have thought of them as poor. Now I see that they are rich and, in God's eyes, truly blessed!

MONDAY 8 APRIL

Poor in Spirit

Matthew 5:1–12

'Blessed are the poor in spirit, for theirs is the kingdom of heaven'
(v. 3, NIV).

We recognise poverty of spirit when we see it but it is hard to capture. 'Poor in spirit' is hard to define. How to explain it? What clothing does it wear? What are its distinctive features? Poverty in spirit is seen in those who are financially poor, such as people who live in city slums or on rubbish mountains, yet who turn out joyful and immaculately dressed for Sunday worship. Poverty of spirit is seen in those who are physically poor, such as people whose deformed feet show the ravages of leprosy, yet who march proudly behind the Salvation Army band at an African congress meeting. Poverty of spirit is seen in those who are intellectually poor, such as the 'special' people, written off by the world as 'mental health patients', who show uncluttered, uncomplaining and unselfconscious love for God and his people.

In saying that the kingdom of heaven belongs to those who are poor in spirit, Jesus surely did not mean that it is only within the reach of those who are financially, physically or intellectually poor. I know a young man who is not poor in any of these ways and yet he has a poverty of spirit that is both warming and welcoming. I suspect it was shaped by hardship and heartache and by finding God when all the other props and masks in his life were stripped away. He lives a life of poverty and piety blended together. His quiet gentleness is not weakness but strength. He's got a lot of living to do yet, but already he holds some of the treasures of the kingdom of heaven in his hands.

Carlo Carretto says, 'God is simple and we make him complicated. He is close to us and we make him far away. The true secret of making contact with God is littleness, simplicity of heart, poverty of spirit – all the things that pride, wealth and cleverness foil in us' (*I Sought and I Found*).

A prayer for today

Lord, show me what it is to be little, simple in heart, poor in spirit.

TUESDAY 9 APRIL

Great Lovers, Great Mourners

Matthew 5:1–12

'Blessed are those who mourn, for they will be comforted'
(v. 4, NIV).

I've come to the conclusion that great lovers make great mourners. What I mean is that the greater the love, the greater the loss and the greater the mourning. Where love is little, then loss is minimal.

I know a couple whose love for each other could only be described as 'exquisite'. It was as beautiful as the china she painted and as strong as the selfless way he cared for her, year after year. They said their wedding vows to each other on a sunny day, long before the vows could be tested. 'I give myself to you,' they said in turn. 'I will love you as long as I have breath.' There were no ifs or buts in this marriage contract, no escape clauses, no loopholes. What they said was what they meant and how they lived for the next fifty-five years.

For a long time their lives were rosy-cheeked with vitality as they worked together, raised a large family and drew others into the embrace of God's love. Then she became unwell and things changed. Well, some things changed. What didn't change was the commitment that he had made to her. Putting his own needs to one side, he cared for her, loving her as God loves. When she died there were no regrets of things not attended to or of love withheld. Just a huge, aching chasm of grief that threatened to engulf him. Such a great loss from such a great love needs a God-sized measure of comfort to wrap around it.

C. S. Lewis said that if we don't want our love to be hurt, then we should wrap it up with little pamperings and luxuries and keep it for ourselves. 'Don't give it away to anyone,' he said, 'not even to an animal.' Thank God that when he offered his love to the world in the person of Jesus, he held nothing back but gave vulnerable, risk-taking love, the sort that those who love and mourn know about 'from the inside'. To great lovers and great mourners today, he offers his great comfort.

WEDNESDAY 10 APRIL

Meekness and Manliness

Matthew 5:1–12

'Blessed are the meek, for they will inherit the earth' (v. 5, NIV).

Meekness has seldom enjoyed a good reputation because it sounds like weakness. Charles Wesley's famous words, 'Gentle Jesus, meek and mild', suggest something colourless and unmanly. The great scholar William Barclay called meekness 'the untranslatable word'. I know a man, however, who translated meekness perfectly into the everyday actions of his life. There was nothing weak or unmanly about him. He was physically slight of build but intellectually a giant. Yet the most memorable thing about him was his gentle spirit. His life was a testimony to the grace of God.

As a youngster he would sit every week on a banana box outside his father's vegetable shop, listening to the Salvation Army open-air meeting. Invited along to the Army Sunday school, he was puzzled when urged to 'give his heart to Jesus' because he knew from school how the heart and lungs worked. He suspected that it would probably mean death. Years later he said, 'When I gave my heart to Jesus, in a sense, I did die.' At a young age he was gripped by the story of David Livingstone and knew that God was calling him, but there were difficulties. Malnourishment and long hours of physical labour resulted in tuberculosis and he spent six months in hospital. His father died, leaving the family homeless and in debt. While the call of God was insistent, the first step was to provide for his mother, and so for years he worked during the day and studied at night until a home was paid for and the debts paid off. He was then free to commence training as a Salvation Army officer.

Officership took him to a large African mission hospital where he was in charge of the medical laboratory, training technicians. It took him out into rural areas where he taught, lived and ate with the African people. He had an insatiable desire to learn and then to pass on what he had learned. Wherever he went, he lived meekness – strength under control, a gentle spirit in the hands of God.

Lord, help me live meekness today.

THURSDAY 11 APRIL
Hungry and Thirsty!

Matthew 5:1–12

'Blessed are those who hunger and thirst for righteousness,
for they will be filled' (v. 6, NIV).

People in Jesus' day believed that riches and plenty were signs of God's favour, but Jesus promised blessing for those who were hungry and thirsty. He made it clear that the poor have an advantage over those who are rich and satisfied. With hands and pockets full, the wealthy can feel no need that their own resources cannot meet. But the poor know they are poor and that they must look to someone beyond themselves to satisfy their needs. To those who are aware of their spiritual poverty and are hungry and thirsty for the things of God, he promised a special blessing of fullness and deep satisfaction.

I have never met anyone so hungry and thirsty for righteous-ness as a woman who arrived in this country with her husband and children after spending eleven years as a refugee. In her earlier years she was a successful busi-nesswoman, hungry and thirsty for money. But when war broke out, she lost everything – her home and her freedom. Shuffled back and forth from one refugee camp to another, she lost an infant son and endured unspeakable treatment, but found the living presence of the Lord Jesus Christ.

Her story is a modern version of Psalm 107. She and her husband 'were hungry and thirsty, and their lives ebbed away. Then they cried out to the LORD in their trouble, and he delivered them from their distress' (Ps 107:5,6). Under the sponsorship of the Salvation Army they came to New Zealand where they now serve as Salvation Army officers. Working with a thriving group of believers, women's groups and young people, she is now passing on her hunger and thirst. Every Saturday a large number of children come to her house, not to play games or watch videos, but to learn Scripture. They practise it on Saturday, then perform it on Sunday. This woman is proving daily that God 'satisfies the thirsty and fills the hungry with good things' (v. 9).

A prayer for today
Lord of loves and longings, create a hunger and thirst in me that will not be lightly satisfied.

FRIDAY 12 APRIL

Pure in Heart

Matthew 5:1–12

'Blessed are the pure in heart, for they will see God' (v. 8, NIV).

When a metal is pure, it is undefiled, unalloyed, unblemished. When a person is pure in heart, they have a singleness of purpose. Søren Kierkegaard described it as 'an integrated life'. 'Purity of heart,' he said, 'is to will one thing.' It is the opposite of ambivalence – being pushed and pulled. It is the corrective to Paul's struggle, 'What I want to do I do not do, but what I hate I do' (*Rom 7:15*). It is echoed in James' call, 'Purify your hearts, you double-minded' (*Jas 4:8*).

When I think of a person who is pure in heart, I think of a woman who, from her commissioning as a Salvation Army officer in 1920 until her promotion to Glory in 1990, lived a consistent, covenanted life with God. At the age of seven she knew that God was calling her. From the age of ten she vowed that she would not do or buy anything unless it would help her as an officer. At fourteen she began to study earnestly, to learn how to testify, to lead services, to prepare Bible messages and to visit the housebound. She was so impressed with *Orders and Regulations for Soldiers* that she determined to learn everything the book contained, and 'worked on it' one chapter at a time.

Her appointments as an officer opened ministry opportunities with women alcoholics, troubled youngsters and cadets in training. In addition to a wide variety of Salvation Army appointments she served tirelessly on countless committees, long after her retirement. She was considered one of the greatest 'campaigners for righteousness' that New Zealand has known. She was a woman pure in heart, single-minded, with one purpose – to make God known. To people like this, the most wonderful promise is given – a long gaze into the very face of God.

People who are pure in heart, however, are not always comfortable to be around. This woman's purity and single-mindedness somehow exposes my divided heart, like a bunch of white roses in a dirty room. So I pray today: King of hearts, I too long to be pure in heart!

SATURDAY 13 APRIL

An Instrument of Peace

Matthew 5:1–12

'Blessed are the peacemakers, for they will be called sons of God'
(v. 9, NIV).

Peacemakers are people who let the peace that is inside them spill over into their world. I know a woman like that. The only child of loving parents, she was shaped in childhood by books and music, growing up with a vision of a world beyond her own. In her late twenties, as a young Salvation Army officer, she set sail for Africa. Her appointment was to Chikankata Institute in Zambia where she was responsible for 150 'upper primary' pupils and a number of teacher trainees. Some of her students found her an enigma. 'Can you be a woman,' one asked her, 'having had no child?' Another commented that her thin legs were not strong enough to hold her up!

Following Zambia's declaration of independence in 1964, she was appointed as headmistress of the renamed Chikankata Secondary School and in charge of 500 students. There was much unrest at that time with students rioting, demanding better food and the expulsion of all expatriate staff. One day she walked into the school compound where the students were making a terrible noise and she shouted as loudly as she could, 'Be quiet!' 'To my surprise,' she said, 'they stopped!'

Staff relationships were another challenge. People from many countries and from a variety of faith backgrounds worked together at the school. 'They became family,' she says, 'but like any family, we had our moments!' That family, now scattered around the world, still looks on this woman as 'Mother', the one the African people called 'Choonde', the counsellor and advisor, the one without whom no important decision can be made. After thirty years of service in Zambia, when news of her retirement reached the villages, some people came to protest. 'Why must you go?' they asked. 'We shall wander in strange forests without you.'

Peacemakers cannot be pretenders. Only peacemakers who are resting their lives on God's peace can make a difference. Real peacemakers are gifts to the world, blessed ones whom God delights to call his sons and daughters.

A prayer for today

Lord, make me an instrument of your peace.

SUNDAY 14 APRIL

When Praise and Petition Stand Side by Side

Psalm 40

'I waited patiently for the LORD; he turned to me and heard my cry . . . Yet I am poor and needy; may the Lord think of me' (vv. 1,17, NIV).

The psalmist knew what it was to live with paradoxes, that is, seeming contradictions. The first eleven verses of Psalm 40 paint a picture of a man standing firm ('my feet on a rock'), singing his song of praise to God ('a new song in my mouth'), finding delight in following the will of God ('your will within my heart'). These sound like days filled with sunshine for the psalmist as he speaks to the congregation of God's righteousness, faithfulness and salvation. May your love and truth always wrap their arms around me in protection, he prays. We say 'Amen', for that is our kind of prayer as well.

At verse 12, however, there is a sudden weather change. The sunshine disappears. His delight turns to despair. Dark words – troubles and sins – sweep in like fog, surrounding him, cutting off his vision. As thick as the fog are those who are 'out to get him', plotting his ruin, taunting him with their mocking words. For a man who so recently felt poised and nurtured, he is now reduced, he says, to being poor and needy (v. 17).

The psalmist speaks of a reality that is all too familiar to believers today. We too are poor and needy. We too know what it is to move from celebration to complaint, from praise to pleading. With every experience of God's life-giving power at work in our lives, there comes a new threat either externally, or from our own shortcomings and sin. We love to be strong, but in reality we too often feel fragile.

At the heart of this psalm, however, there is a glimmer of hope. The writer to the Hebrews puts the words of sacrifice and offering (vv. 6–8) into the mouth of Jesus (see *Heb 10:5–7*). All the sacrifices required under Mosaic law, and familiar to the psalmist, have been replaced by the sacrifice of Jesus. For a people poor and needy, delighting and despairing, Jesus has made a once-and-for-all, permanent sacrifice that declares our freedom and forgiveness, even in the midst of the paradoxes of life.

JOGGING WITH JAMES
Introduction

Mary, you've been on my mind a lot lately. I've been remembering how we first met, and giving thanks to God for that work placement that brought you here for four weeks. You looked so nervous on your first day as you told me that you couldn't stand people yelling at you. You'd had enough of that in your childhood, you said. I was glad to assure you that while you worked here, no one would yell at you! You showed so much interest in the Salvation Army that, when I invited you along to a Sunday meeting, you almost jumped for joy! I recall the day, not many weeks later, when you knelt at the place of prayer and asked Jesus Christ to take control of your life.

I loved the way you soaked up the teaching in the recruits' class, and I will never forget the day you were enrolled. Wow! The hall was packed. There was the usual Sunday crowd and, as well, all your friends from the local club. They were delighted to be there and so proud of you! You looked terrific in your new uniform and everyone was moved to hear the testimony of what God has done in your life.

We've walked and talked together a lot since then, Mary. It's been wonderful to watch you grow as a Christian, and your freshness and exuberance for the things of God have been a real blessing – and at times a rebuke – to me. I know there are some things you struggle with and some things you don't understand. So, I've had an idea! Instead of just chatting about the weather or last evening's TV programmes as we go for our daily walk, what say we invite James, one of the New Testament authors, to come along with us, and to teach us both what it means to be a Christian in this twenty-first century? We could call it 'jogging with James'! What do you think of the idea, Mary?

MONDAY 15 APRIL
Who, When, Why?

James 1:1

'James, a servant of God and of the Lord Jesus Christ, to the twelve tribes scattered among the nations: Greetings' (v. 1, NIV).

James, I'd like you to meet my friend Mary. She's a colourful person, generous, warm-hearted, and really keen to learn. She grew up in a society marked by superstition. The baby born before her died, so when Mary was born, her mother gave her away, thinking that that would appease the gods. Mary was not registered at birth, so she could not go to school, and she grew up feeling like a 'non-person'. She spent most of her childhood in an orphanage where religion was measured out like a daily dose of medicine. Recently, Mary became a Christian and is discovering to her surprise that God is not angry and vengeful, as she grew up believing. We're looking into your letter, James, to find some guidelines for being a follower of Jesus.

Mary, I'd like you to meet James. James was one of Jesus' brothers. Imagine growing up in the same household as Jesus, playing with him, fixing things, and doing things together as brothers like to do. I wonder if James was among the family group who came to take Jesus away (*Mark 3:31*). If he didn't understand Jesus' mission then, he must have understood it later – perhaps at the cross, or when Jesus appeared to him after the resurrection (*1 Cor 15:7*) – because he became a leader in the church at Jerusalem (*Acts 15:13*). His letter is dated around AD 49 and is considered one of the earliest of all the New Testament writings.

He writes to Jewish Christians who have been scattered by persecution throughout the Mediterranean world, addressing his readers as a preacher addresses his hearers – directly, straight to the point. He writes to encourage them and to remind them that genuine faith is not just a matter of words, or a doctrinal statement, but a living faith that shows itself in action.

This man, Mary, is talking our language. His teaching about trials and temptations, watching the way we speak and the dangers of wealth all has a very modern sound to it. I think we're in for some solid and helpful learning!

TUESDAY 16 APRIL
A Fresh Look at Trials

James 1:2–8

'Consider it pure joy, my brothers, whenever you face trials of many kinds' (v. 2, NIV).

As he writes to believers who have been scattered by persecution, James begins in a rather startling way, telling them to rejoice because of their trials. 'Consider yourselves fortunate', he says (*GNB*). Now you're no stranger to hard times, Mary. You've told me some of the tough things that happened to you when you were growing up. How would you feel if someone told you to be joyful for those experiences?

Yet James tells his readers to welcome their trials for the simple reason that the testing of their faith will develop perseverance and that's the mark of someone who is serious about living the Christian life. He links perseverance with maturity. That's a better word than 'perfection'. Many believers think that to be perfect, one has to be wrapped around with a kind of protective layer that sin cannot penetrate. But let's not forget that God has made us human, and it's the glorious mixture of good and bad, success and failure, light and shade, that he loves.

I'm glad James uses the word 'mature' because it means being fully what God intended us to be.

It's a word full of potential, an invitation to keep pressing on, even when we do fall. James says that if we need wisdom to understand the tough times we are going through, all we need to do is ask God for insight and he will give it to us, not in a stingy way, but generously and without condemning us.

I read about a woman who was imprisoned in the Nazi concentration camp at Ravensbruck. In that terrible place, she could easily have given in to despair. But the wisdom of God enabled her to see her situation not as misfortune, but as opportunity. She wrote, 'I am thy message, Lord. Throw me, like a blazing torch into the night, so that all may see and understand what it means to be thy disciple.'

Mary, let's turn today's tough moments into an opportunity to persevere!

WEDNESDAY 17 APRIL

Trials and Temptations

James 1:12–18

'Blessed is the man who perseveres under trial, because when he
has stood the test, he will receive the crown of life that God
has promised to those who love him' (v. 12, NIV).

When writing about trials and temptations, James uses the same word in Greek to describe them both, but makes a distinction between trials as something to be endured (*vv. 2–11*) and temptations as something to be avoided (*vv. 13,14*). This is a topic we've often discussed, Mary.

In the first part of the chapter, he writes about trials as opportunities for the growth of character and spiritual maturity. Take, for example, the hard times when we have to wait for something. We have two options. Either we scream and vent our frustration, or else we see the waiting as an opportunity to learn patience. So, James is saying, trials equal opportunity to persevere and to mature.

But a trial becomes a temptation when we give in to its wrong and then blame someone or something else for the consequences. You have heard the excuses people make: 'The devil made me do it' or 'I had a dysfunctional childhood' or 'My father was an alcoholic, so I knew no better.' Worst of all, says James, is when we blame God for tempting us. Tread carefully here, he says. God does allow us to go through hard times, to test and refine our faith, but he will never lead us into sin. We ourselves do that. Even when we become Christians there is still a capacity within us to make wrong choices. We may think about something that isn't really evil, but nor is it holy. It might feel quite innocent, just a little playing with the thought in our mind, a little fondling of its possibilities. 'But beware,' James says. 'You're like a fish that is lured by a tasty bait and about to be snared.'

Mary, being human means that we cannot avoid tough times. But whether they are trials that lead us to spiritual maturity, or temptations that lead us into sin, it all depends on the way we handle them. No wonder Jesus suggested this phrase in his prayer: 'Keep us safe from ourselves and the Devil' (*Matt 6:12, The Message*).

That's my prayer for today, Mary.

THURSDAY 18 APRIL
Words, Words, Words

James 1:19–27

'If anyone considers himself religious and yet does not keep a tight rein on his tongue, he deceives himself and his religion is worthless' (v. 26, NIV).

I happened to glance over to you during the service on Sunday, Mary, and felt moved to see the way you were concentrating on what the preacher was saying. You were really drinking it in. I've noticed too the well-worn look your Bible is getting as you underline significant words and phrases. And I can be sure that if there is an opportunity to request a song, your choice will be 'Amazing Grace'.

One thing that James emphasises in his letter, Mary, is the importance of not just hearing, or speaking, or even singing the words of the faith, but actually doing them. He has a lot to say about words, and how important it is to listen before we speak. You know the old saying about having two ears and one mouth, so that we can listen twice as much as we speak! James knew that words can be used to hurt and to heal. Anger, gossip, slander, arguments – none of these helps anyone to grow in righteousness. But when we listen with humility, our words can then be an encouragement and blessing to others.

This attitude of humility is in fact one of the characteristics of being a Christian. It's related to the word 'humus', meaning 'earth', and is a recognition of our earthiness in relation to God's wisdom. Humility is the attitude with which we receive God's word and allow it to take root and flourish in our lives. If we just listen to God's word, but do not put it into practice, James says that it is like catching a glimpse of ourselves in the mirror, then turning away and forgetting what we look like. But when we look into the mirror of God's law, and act on what we see, then we are blessed.

James tells it straight. Religion that is just words is worthless. We are to mirror God's character, care for those who are powerless, give without expecting a return, and live a godly life in a godless world.

Mary, we can only do this by his amazing grace!

FRIDAY 19 APRIL
So Who Is God's Favourite?

James 2:1–13

'Has not God chosen those who are poor in the eyes of the world to be rich in faith and to inherit the kingdom he promised those who love him?' (v. 5, NIV).

Mary, I heard about a woman who moved to a new town and couldn't decide which church to link up with. There were two places of worship to choose from, so she did an experiment. On her first Sunday, she dressed up in designer clothes, jewellery, make-up, the lot. She went along to one church and noticed the way she was welcomed and treated. The next Sunday she dressed up as a 'bag-lady' with her hair dishevelled, her clothes tatty and with a few supermarket bags containing strange items! Again, she took note of how she was treated. On the following two Sundays she repeated the experiment at the other church in town.

Her findings were remarkable. At the first church, on the Sunday when she was all dressed up, she was welcomed warmly, but the next week she was totally ignored. At the second church, people stood back a little and eyed her in her finery. On her second Sunday there, she was welcomed by a number of people and even embraced by a woman who offered to carry her bags! You can probably guess which church she chose to join!

James has some stern things to say about favouritism. He has already told us that true religion is shown in one's care of orphans and widows, those who have no rights or standing (1:27). Now he says quite bluntly that if we judge people by their outward appearance and honour the rich but dishonour the poor, then we are actually sinning against God. In God's eyes, Mary, there are no 'haves' and 'have-nots'. He treats everyone as equals, although if he were into favourites, they would be the poor and the powerless. Jesus himself declared that the poor in spirit, those who show an attitude of humble trust in God, are the blessed ones (Matt 5:3). The real heart of the matter, after all, is the matter of the heart!

Let's look out for new people in our service this Sunday, Mary. There could be someone dressed in riches or rags who is really a seeker in disguise!

SATURDAY 20 APRIL
Putting Faith into Action

James 2:14–26

'Faith by itself, if it is not accompanied by action, is dead'
(v. 17, NIV).

Do you remember a young woman coming into our Sunday evening service a few months ago, Mary? It was a very wet night and she was cold and distressed. She poured out her story to Mrs A. who met her at the door, saying that she had come because she knew that 'Army people help people'. Mrs A. took her home, rang her family, and looked after her for a few days until she felt ready to go back home. I'm so glad, Mary, that that young woman found that her trust in 'Army people' proved true that evening.

James would agree fully. In his practical, straight-to-the-point manner, he says that being a Christian is not just a matter of quoting the doctrines correctly or knowing certain biblical facts. Real Christianity is a matter of putting faith into action.

He uses the example of two champions of the faith. He quotes Abraham who was told by God to go and sacrifice his son as an offering (*Gen 22*). It didn't seem to make sense to slaughter the boy for whom he had prayed and waited so long, but Abraham trusted God. As it happened, God provided another sacrifice, but Abraham had shown that he had faith in God and was fully prepared to act on it. Likewise, the prostitute Rahab, a Canaanite woman, showed her faith in the God of Israel by giving shelter to the spies who were checking out the promised land (*Josh 2*).

This is really the heart of James' letter, Mary. We are saved by faith (*Eph 2:8*), which is God's gift and grace to us. But we show that we are saved by how we live and act towards others. If there is no action, then it's not genuine faith. In fact, faith without action, says James, is as dead as a body without a spirit.

This is 'Christianity with its sleeves rolled up', Mary, the kind of faith-in-action that the Salvation Army is known for. Let's keep our eyes and ears open today for someone who may be in need.

SUNDAY 21 APRIL

A Prayer for a Sick Person

Psalm 41

'In my integrity you uphold me and set me in your presence forever'
(v. 12, NIV).

The first Book of Psalms concludes, as it began, with a 'Blessed' psalm. Psalm 41 is the song of both lament and thanksgiving of a sick person who has come to the temple to seek God's healing. Before he speaks, however, he must hear a statement from the priest concerning the basic character of the kind of person who is qualified to ask for God's blessing and healing. Such a person, the priest announces, is one who has taken care of the needs of the weak. Anyone who has done that may then seek God's blessing in his own time of weakness. 'The LORD will sustain . . . and restore him' (v. 3).

Having heard the priest's declaration, the sick person makes his peace with God. Aware of both his sin and his sickness, he asks for divine mercy, which will bring *shalom*, wholeness, to both body and soul. He then expresses words of lament. Like vultures circling over a dying animal, his enemies hover round him, waiting for him to die. Visitors come to see him and speak the usual pleasantries, but in his heart he imagines the things they say to each other as they leave.

The greatest betrayal of all, however, is that the good friend with whom he shared many moments of fellowship has 'lifted up his heel' against him.

His lament is bracketed by prayer (*vv. 4,10–12*). Once again he asks for mercy and healing and, as he prays, he receives the assurance of God's acceptance of his prayer. He will once more stand in the presence of God. This may refer to future visits to the temple for worship, but it is also a word of thanks that God has spared him from the threat of death that came so close. Verse 13 is a doxology. With one voice, the worshipping community lifts up their song of praise, their 'Amen' to the psalms of this book, which have taken them on a journey through sin and sorrow, forgiveness and restoration.

To reflect on
Do you catch a glimpse of Jesus in this psalm?

Taming the Tongue

James 3:1–12

'The tongue is a small part of the body, but it makes great boasts'
(v. 5, NIV).

Have you noticed that new office block being built just along from the Army hall, Mary? I understand it will be some months before the building is complete and ready for occupation. Within less than a day, the little cottage on the site was levelled and the rubble trucked away, a lifetime of memories removed in just a few hours. Watching that happen reminded me of James' teaching about the power of the tongue to build up and to destroy.

James sounds a warning to those who want to be teachers. He knew that in Jewish culture, and in the early church, the position of teacher was one of high status with a power of influence. In fact, he says, for all of us – teachers, leaders or whoever we are – our words have power. He likens the tongue to a bit in the mouth of a horse, or a rudder that guides a ship. These things are small but they are the control mechanism of the horse, the ship, the body, and as such need to be used with great care.

The uncontrolled tongue, he says, is like a small fire – just a spark, a tiny flame – that can set a whole forest ablaze with destructive power, killing everything in its path and leaving a blackened scar on the landscape for years afterwards. A word of gossip or slander, a subtle exaggeration, a verbal 'stab-in-the-back' can do the same kind of damage, destroying a person's integrity or wrecking a relationship that may take years to rebuild. This kind of tongue, says James, is from the very pit of hell itself, a restless evil, full of deadly poison. He says that the tongue is used both to bless God and curse others, our fellow human beings, who have been made in God's likeness. Such contradictory speech is as unnatural as a fig tree growing olives, or a salt spring producing fresh water.

Mary, this is my prayer for today:
'May the words of my mouth and the meditation of my heart be pleasing in your sight, O Lord' (Ps 19:14).

TUESDAY 23 APRIL
Two Kinds of Wisdom

James 3:13–18

'Who is wise and understanding among you? Let him show it by his good life, by deeds done in the humility that comes from wisdom' (v. 13, NIV).

Mary, you might not use the word 'wise' to describe yourself, but I think it is a very apt description. You've told me about your harsh upbringing and the things you had to do to make your way in life. I suspect you've always had firm beliefs and a keen eye to observe and 'read' other people. Some would describe you as 'worldly-wise' or 'street-smart', but I suspect you've had to be like that in order to survive.

Now that you've become a Christian, Mary, a whole new world of wisdom is opening up to you – God's wisdom. James helpfully explains it, contrasting it with the worldly sort. We need to remember that he was writing to believers who had been scattered by persecution. Some of the teaching they were receiving was worldly rather than godly wisdom.

In describing worldly wisdom, he says that it is earthly (that is, at odds with God), unspiritual (without the touch of God upon it) and demonic (inspired by the devil himself). Strong words! This kind of wisdom says 'Look out for Number One', or 'If it feels good, do it', or 'Get to the top, no matter who you have to climb over to get there.' People could say that these are survival slogans for a scattered people, Mary, but they are opposed to what God calls us to.

In contrast, the wisdom of God (James calls it 'the wisdom that comes from heaven') is pure (with unmixed motives), peace-loving (creating a peace-making spirit), considerate (calmly working for justice), submissive (gentle and reasonable), full of mercy (evidenced by acts of kindness) and good fruit (seen in loving deeds), impartial (singular in purpose) and sincere (without hypocrisy). That's quite a list, Mary!

James ends his description of godly wisdom by likening peacemakers to sowers who plant seeds of peace and raise a harvest of righteousness. Any claim to wisdom will always be tested by the results it produces.

Mary, let's live today, by God's help, in the 'humility that comes from wisdom' (v. 13).

WEDNESDAY 24 APRIL
A Wake-Up Call

James 4:1–6

'God opposes the proud but gives grace to the humble' (v. 6, NIV).

James has used some strong words in this letter, Mary, but he is not finished yet! In his fourth chapter he returns to the problem of the tongue, and describes the lethal effects of the tongue under the influence of false wisdom. He paints a picture of a fellowship of believers deeply divided, filled with jealousy, selfish ambition and quarrels. There's a battle going on within you, he says, meaning both within the individual believers and within the whole Christian community. As in a tug of war, they are being pulled one way by conscience, another way by evil desires.

They want status or, rather, what they hope status will bring them – namely a sense of wholeness, joy and peace. But James says they won't get it because they are looking in the wrong place. They should ask God for his wisdom (1:5) and they will discover that his wisdom also brings with it the wholeness and peace they long for. Your prayers are not being answered, James says, for three reasons:

• You are not asking God.
• You are asking for the wrong things.
• You are asking with the wrong motives.

Their prayers are marked by their desire for 'pleasures' rather than by a willingness to put themselves into God's hands and to be moulded and shaped by him. James loves these believers but he calls them adulterous people, lovers of pleasure rather than lovers of God, as Paul puts it (2 Tim 3:4). James sounds like an Old Testament prophet who wants his readers to wake up, rub the sleep from their eyes, look in the mirror (1:23) and see themselves as they really are. Their desire for status and wealth is not only causing division within them, it is also taking them away from God. But while God's demands may seem harsh, he always provides the strength and grace for those who put their trust in him.

Mary, I wonder if James holds a key for us as to why at times our prayers are not answered. What do you think?

THURSDAY 25 APRIL
A Recipe for Humility

James 4:6–12

'Humble yourselves before the Lord, and he will lift you up'
(v. 10, NIV).

Mary, our discussion about humility a couple of days ago raised the question of how one becomes humble. We might have known that the ever-practical James, having described 'the wisdom that comes from humility' would not leave us in the dark as to how it can be cultivated. He reminds us that God gives grace to the humble and then lists the steps that we need to take. It is a list full of movement, towards God, away from the evil, inwards to oneself and then outwards to others. Let's look at the list.

- *Submit to God.* This is James' call to repentance, a change of direction made with a humble and contrite spirit. Whenever we come to God in this way, we are embraced by his forgiveness.
- *Resist the devil.* James may have been thinking of Jesus' dealings with the devil in the desert, which put him to flight, at least for a time (*Luke 4:13*). James had no doubt that the devil is the source of all evil and must be deliberately opposed.

- *Come near to God.* In contrast, James urges us to turn towards God. As we do that, we find that God turns towards us. This is the God whom Jesus portrayed as a loving, ever-watchful father waiting for his prodigal son.
- *Wash your hands, purify your hearts.* James sounds like the psalmist who urged that both the inner being and the outer actions must be cleansed (*Ps 24:4*).
- *Grieve, mourn and wail.* These are strong words, urging us to take sin seriously.
- *Change laughter to mourning and joy to gloom.* James reminds his readers that the pursuit of wealth and status will not lead to true joy.
- *Humble yourselves before the Lord.* True wholeness and joy will be found nowhere else but in God.
- *Do not slander or judge.* It's fine to observe, but when we judge someone else, we are breaking God's law of love.

So there it is, Mary, a recipe for humility. Which ingredient should we start working on today?

Making Profit, Making Plans

James 4:13–17

'Instead, you ought to say, "If it is the Lord's will, we will live and do this or that" ' (v. 15, NIV).

'Now listen,' says James. I can imagine him pulling up a chair, Mary, and looking his audience right in the eye. 'This is important.' He's heard that some of the merchants and traders within the Christian community are talking about their plans to travel to various places and set up business. There's nothing wrong with that on the surface, but James challenges them for setting plans in motion with no reference to God. Their desire to make a profit is all that matters to them.

The parable of the rich fool comes to mind (*Luke 12:16–21*), the man who thought he had everything he needed, but left God out of the picture. More pertinently, James may have been thinking of the merchants who, in the words of Amos, trample on the needy as they anxiously await the end of the Sabbath so that they can make more money (*Amos 8:4–6*).

James condemns the smug, self-satisfied attitude that counts the making of a fortune as more important than devotion to God. These are wealthy people whom he is addressing, and as members of the Christian community they have a responsibility to see their wealth as God-given and use it accordingly. These could be the same people who have shown favouritism to the wealthy and a condescending attitude to the poor (*2:1–4*).

In spite of their boastful plans, all of which are in the future tense, the future is uncertain. Their life is like a mist that vanishes in a moment. Hosea spoke about people who had turned from God and said they were like 'the early dew that disappears' (*Hos 13:3*). James uses the same image, saying that when the future is uncertain, the key is to trust in God's graciousness, not in human plans. God must be in control of our plans and when he is not, then any boasting about our accomplishments is simply evil. Now that you know what is right, he concludes, just do it!

Mary, here's a promise for today:
'Commit to the LORD whatever you do, and your plans will succeed' (Prov 16:3).

SATURDAY 27 APRIL

A Warning to the Rich

James 5:1–6

'Now listen, you rich people, weep and wail because of the misery that is coming upon you' (v. 1, NIV).

'Now listen,' James says again, shifting his focus from the merchants to landowners. Suddenly the pastor sounds more like an Old Testament prophet warning his readers about a coming day of destruction. The landowners are suffering from the same affliction as the merchants – an insatiable desire for and trust in wealth. Like Jeremiah or Ezekiel calling their people to repentance, James tells the rich to weep and wail in remorse and grief. The misery they are about to endure is a result of the misuse of their wealth. They have used it for themselves, living 'in luxury and self-indulgence', instead of using it to alleviate the sufferings of the poor. In fact, their very desire for wealth has caused suffering, in the meagre wages or no wages at all that they have paid to the slaves and free poor men who work for them.

All this greed, however, has done them no good. Their wealth, the stored produce of the land, has rotted. Moths have eaten their fine clothing. Their gold and silver have corroded. With the eye of a prophet, James sees these future events as though they have already happened. An even more serious heart corrosion has happened. Their trust in their wealth has caused them to sin against their brothers and sisters. They will be judged and condemned for their selfishness and murderous abuse of power. They have kept adding to their material hoard like cattle fattening themselves, not realising that the day of slaughter is upon them.

This is strong language, Mary, and we might well wonder what it has to say to us today. Neither of us is wealthy, or in a position of power. But the question is, how do we use what we do have? Let's remember that Jesus said our treatment of the poor, the prisoner, the thirsty, is really our treatment of him (*Matt 25:31–46*).

'Money has a dangerous way of putting scales on one's eyes, a dangerous way of freezing people's hands, eyes, lips and hearts.'

Dom Heldert Camara

SUNDAY 28 APRIL
A Song of Tears

Psalm 42

'Why are you downcast, O my soul? Why so disturbed within me?
Put your hope in God, for I will yet praise him, my Saviour and my
God' (v. 11, NIV).

If the psalms were all songs with happy endings, we would sing them on sunny days, but dismiss them as irrelevant on days when depression wraps its cold fingers around our heart. Psalm 42 is a very human psalm, a song of tears by one who feels abandoned by God. The psalmist, exiled from his homeland or prevented from attending worship because of illness, is like a thirsty animal in a dry place. He thirsts for God and especially the worship of God in the temple, but all he tastes is the bitter water of tears.

'Where is your God?' he is asked. The question sounds like the mocking taunt of his enemies who voice what he fears – that God has departed. Feeling deserted and despairing, he determines to recall the times when he went with a great crowd of pilgrims to the temple in Jerusalem to participate in the worship festivals. He led the procession himself, indicating that his role in the liturgy was signifi-cant. He remembers but he is still downcast and praise is still distant.

The psalm's refrain, 'Why are you downcast, O my soul?' leads him to determine once more to call upon the rich store of memory. 'I will remember you' (v. 6), he says. This time he recalls, not the pilgrim crowds or the festivals, but God himself. He remembers places where he has known and experi-enced the presence of God in the past. But as he thinks of the great mountain range and the ocean, it is as if the very waters of the deep break in chaos over him. He is a man overwhelmed with grief, forgotten and abandoned by God, taunted by his enemies. Twice he remembers, but still he is down-cast. Like a drowning man he grabs hold of one slim thread of hope – 'I will yet praise him.' The psalmist feeds on tears, day and night (v. 3). Day and night, the Lord directs his song of love towards him (v. 8).

Today and tonight, listen to the sound of the song of love that God sings to you.

MONDAY 29 APRIL
A Call to Patience

James 5:7–12

'Be patient, then, brothers, until the Lord's coming. See how the farmer waits for the land to yield its valuable crop and how patient he is for the autumn and spring rains' (v. 7, NIV).

As James begins to bring his letter to a close, he returns to calling his readers 'brothers'. Although he has had some harsh words of rebuke to say to them, he is still their brother in Christ. He now turns from the wealthy to the poor with a call to patience. By way of illustration, he describes a farmer who waits patiently for harvest time and for the autumn and spring rains. Mary, like me you've lived in a country with a long dry season and a short rainy season, and you know how vital that rain is for the success of the crops and the health of the people.

In the same way, believers must wait patiently for the coming of the Lord. Such waiting can be hard, for there is no knowing just when he will return. But, as for the farmer, there is work to be done in the waiting time. Difficulties must be dealt with, relationships nurtured, teaching maintained, faith encouraged and expressed in action. Every day of waiting has its work of patience and devotion to do.

James had stern words to say to the rich, but he has a warning for the poor as well. In spite of the suffering they have endured at the hands of the wealthy, they should not grumble against each other. A complaining spirit does not lead to peace, nor does it solve anything. They need to remember that even the wealthy are sisters and brothers, fellow believers in Christ. Only the Lord himself has the right to judge.

As a further example of patience he quotes the Old Testament prophets and Job who endured, patiently waiting for the judgment and mercy of God. Blessed are such people, he says, repeating what Jesus himself said (*Matt 5:10–12*). Above all, he concludes, don't let your impatience trap you into using God's name in a flippant way. Let your words be honest and straightforward – 'yes' when you mean 'yes' and 'no' when you mean 'no'.

Mary, how would you and I live today if we knew Jesus was coming back tomorrow?

TUESDAY 30 APRIL
The Prayer of Faith

James 5:12–20

'The prayer of a righteous man is powerful and effective'
(v. 16, NIV).

James' closing words have to do with prayer – an individual's prayer (v. 13), the prayer of the elders for the sick (vv. 14,15), the prayers of friends and companions for one another (v. 16) and the prayer of the righteous prophet Elijah (vv. 17,18). Mary, let me tell you about one incident that makes this passage very meaningful for me.

When my husband and I were in Zambia, our daughter was just a baby and often unwell. We lived on the same compound as Chikankata Hospital and had expert care available to us. Late one night I told my husband how anxious I was about her. We picked her up, read these words from James, anointed her with ordinary cooking oil and asked God to heal her. We didn't ask him for a miracle, nor did we tell him what he had to do. We simply gave her back to God, placing her trustingly in his arms. Some time later, our wonderful doctor discovered that she had a hole in the heart. Another year later, back home in New Zealand, the hole was corrected, just stitched up, said the surgeon, making it sound as easy as mending a pair of socks!

People wondered at that time how we could be so calm, but we told them we had dealt with that matter, two years earlier.

There have been many times since then, Mary, when I have prayed for people in need of God's healing. Sometimes they are healed and sometimes not. It is a mystery. But every time someone is prayed for, I believe something of their load is lifted. A sense of peace comes in place of their anxiety or fear. Even medical science is agreeing now that when people pray and ask for divine help, something positive happens.

Well, there it is, Mary. We've walked a long way with James over the past couple of weeks. I hope you've found his handbook on Christianity helpful. May God bless you as you keep on putting your faith into action, making your world an outpost of heaven!

INDEX

(as from: Advent 1996)

Words of Life Bible reading notes
are published three times a year:

Easter
(January–April)

Pentecost
(May–August)

Advent
(September–December)

In each edition you will find:

- informative commentary
- a wide variety of Bible passages
- topics for praise and prayer
- points to ponder
- cross references for further study

Why not place a regular order for *Words of Life*?
Collect each volume and build a lasting resource
for personal or group study.